MW00616066

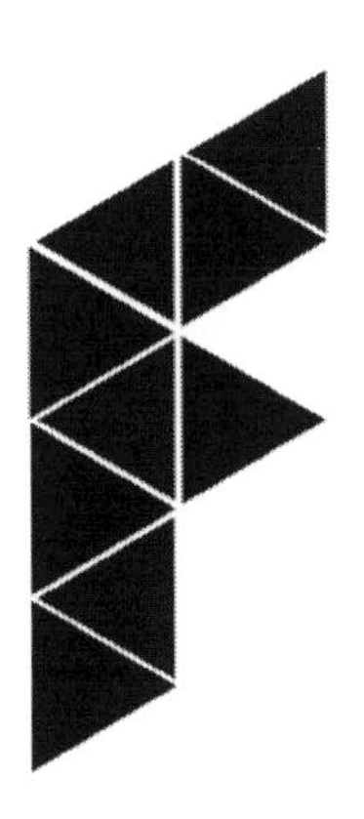

FUSION

CHILDREN'S MINISTRY

BOOK THREE: CULTURE, PERSPECTIVES, PASTORAL MINISTRY

Created by the Northwest Ministry Network:
Brent Colby, Lauren Beach, Nick Caalim,
Dave M. Cameron, Jessica Downs, Dorene Heeter,
Dan Metteer, Jace Murray, and Bryan Reeder

Northwest Ministry Network
35131 SE Douglas St. #200
Snoqualmie WA 98065
www.nwministry.com

To Mel:

Your work is our reward.

Our reward is to work with others.

CONTENTS

INTRODUCTION

fu·sion /ˈfyo͞oZHən
The process or result of joining two or more
things together to form a single entity.

Children's ministry is one of the greatest and most difficult things that you will ever do. It is great because it has such a powerful influence on the lives of individuals; our experiences as children shape the types of adults we will become. It is hard because it requires a glorious amount of work in the most un-glorious circumstances. This book is designed to help you focus on the ideas that are most critical to the success of children's ministry in your own church. It is not a book of answers, but rather, a book of ideas and a book of questions. *Fusion: Children's Ministry* is designed to help you think about some of the most critical aspects of children's ministry today. God never intended for you to do this alone. So let's do this together and see what it takes to lead an entire generation to Jesus.

If you're reading this book, then I assume you have something to do with the children's ministry in your own church. Let me be the first to congratulate you and say that you have one of the most important jobs in the world today. The future of the church will rise or fall on the shoulders of children's ministry, and you get to play a crucial part. No pressure.

What Is at Stake

We are living in a unique stage of Church history and have a unique opportunity to influence the future. For generations, the

Church has assumed a central role Western society. The influence of the Church began to wane decades ago. A rising tide has become a flood and the biblical worldview has been washed out of popular culture. Our society praises selfishness over sacrifice, dysfunction over discipline, and tolerance over truth. We are told that the Christian point of view is ignorant, backward, and bigoted. And therein lies our great advantage: The message of the gospel is needed more now than ever. And what better place to proclaim the truth than in the lives of *the least of these.* The ideas you think, the teams you lead, and the work you do will have a profound impact on the future. Are you up for the challenge?

What this Book Is About

This book has been designed to present a series of big ideas surrounding the world of children's ministry. It is organized around three themes including culture, perspectives, and pastoral ministry. This is a collaborative book, which means that each chapter has been written by a different author. That's right, each of us is writing from our own perspective and from our own experiences. One thing we do share is this: we want to help you lead a more effective ministry to kids and parents.

Who are "we?" Good question. We are a group of children's pastors throughout the Pacific Northwest with a heart for ministry leaders. Each of us is different and we serve in very different churches. Some of us are paid, others are volunteer. Some of our churches are over 100 years old, others were just planted a few years ago. Some of us work with paid staff, while others don't get paid themselves. The thing you should know is this: our churches are real and our ideas have been shaped one weekend at a time. This book is not just about good ideas or concepts; this is a book with proven tactics and insight that can improve your ability to lead children and families in your own church.

This book contains some great ideas about children's ministry. More importantly, it asks you some great questions at the end of each chapter. How you answer these questions can transform the way in which you lead parents and kids closer to Jesus. I encourage you to read this book with others; don't read it alone. Spend some time working through the questions at the end of each chapter.

How It Is Organized

Spoiler alert: we will be discussing children's ministry as it relates to three areas: popular culture, past and future perspectives, and pastoral ministry. This is the third book in a series that also addresses the areas of leadership, theology, environments, science, science, and families. If you missed out on the first two books, search the internet for *Fusion: Children's Ministry,* Books One and Two.

The themes will be covered by a series of chapters designed to challenge the way you think about a topic. The ideas at the end of the chapter are for you to discuss with others. Remember, these are the ideas of individual children's pastors. You don't have to agree with everything we say. But we do ask that you think about these ideas for yourself and decide what is best for you and your church.

It's time for you to stop doing children's ministry alone. It's time for you to start doing children's ministry better. We hope that this book will help you accomplish those goals. Now turn the page and get to work.

PART SEVEN: CULTURE

Culture has become a powerful word that sums up the whole of human existence. When we think of culture there are few things that we *do not* think of. Culture refers to all types of entertainment including music, television, and film. Culture also refers to values including traditional, liberal, and everything in between. Culture refers to fashion, language, traditions, and pipe organs. Yes, one of the most powerful culture clashes I have ever experienced was centered around the existence of a pipe organ.

If you have been serving in the church long then I am sure that this battle royal has come to your town as well. One group loves the organ, another group thinks that it is simply taking up space on the stage. The two groups clash over what Jesus would have wanted, comfortably ignoring the fact that the organ wasn't invented until 300 years after his resurrection.

We know that churches can serve and follow Jesus with or without pipe organs. Our choice of "joyful noisemaker" may be amoral. But there are many aspects of culture that have a definite bearing on the human soul; how do we determine when and how to interact with aspects of popular culture today?

This part of the book addresses the church's relationship with culture. It includes discussions of consumerism, the relationship between ministry and childcare, as well as the role of popular culture in the local church.

7.1 CONSUMER CULTURE AND CHILDREN'S MINISTRY

Brent Colby

Let's get one thing clear: breakfast is the best meal of the day. Lunch and dinner are great, but breakfast takes the cake; pancake. Close your eyes with me, now open them so you can read. Can you smell the bacon, eggs, and sausage? Can you taste the orange juice and coffee? Now walk with me down the supermarket hall of fame known as the cereal aisle. Grocers have dedicated an entire aisle to the celebration that is breakfast cereal. There is no better way to break your fast than with a savory or sweet first meal of the day. The only thing better than breakfast itself is breakfast for dinner.

As a kid, I wanted few things more than to have breakfast for dinner. I would trade casseroles for crepes any day of the week. My father was the greatest advocate for postmeridian pancakes and I proudly follow in his footsteps. I think this is what Benjamin Franklin had in mind when he said, "don't put off until tomorrow what you can do today." Today, I can eat breakfast whenever I want.

As Westerners, we are accustomed to having a great number of choices. If you want breakfast for dinner, then it is yours. Many restaurants allow you to order bacon and eggs around the clock. But this free market extends beyond the meals we eat; it also applies to the things we buy. Take peanut butter, for example. Do you want smooth, crunchy, extra crunchy, organic, or stir-free? And remember to choose between almond butter, sesame butter, and soy butter. Name brand? Check. Store brand? Check. Don't forget the variety of sizes ranging from thimble to tub.

But maybe you have a nut allergy and want to buy a television instead. Be sure to figure out what resolution, size, and refresh rate you are looking for. Are you interested in HD, 4KUHD, LED, HDR, 3D, or OLED? Do you want to buy a television that is flat or curved? Smart or dumb? Perhaps you want a display thin enough to slice bread? All of these options are available and we have come to expect nothing less.

Defining Consumer Culture

It's a shopper's world out there and we are all buying it. Today we buy much more than food and electronics. We are also connoisseurs of ideas, experiences, and identities. The advertisements that you see on the television, hear on the radio, and click online are selling you more than ever before. We know that beer can't sell you friends, insurance can't sell you confidence, and a truck can't sell you manliness. However, this does not stop millions of people from buying these things every day. As consumers we don't just want to buy a thing, we want to buy *into a thing* and all that it represents. That is to say: people aren't shopping for stuff; they are shopping for meaning.

Aggressive marketing has become an inescapable part of our society. Wherever you turn, it's there and it's not going away. Capitalism doesn't just ask us to make stuff, it asks us to sell that stuff for a profit as well.[1] This system inspired the creation of the Model T, Mickey Mouse, and the iPhone. When Henry, Walt, and Steve began selling to us, our value system began to change. In many cases, family and faith have been undersold by phones and Fords. Now, children's pastors compete with the schemes of the devil and Disney all at the same time (no offense, Mickey). We are being asked to win spiritual wars on commercial battlefronts. Are you teaching biblical literacy, fostering spiritual depth, and creating cooler environments than Legoland?

This problem is not limited to the kids themselves; young parents have also been caught up in this new world of consumerism. Neil Howe and Will Strauss describe the current generation of young parents as a, "consumer behemoth, riding atop a new youth economy of astounding scale and extravagance."[2] Adults are addicted to their screens and check their cell phones in excess of forty-six times a day.[3] Some critics argue that the cell phone addictions run much deeper than this. They accuse young parents of, "constantly pressing levers to get tiny pellets of social or intellectual nourishment."[4] And how are these young adults parenting their kids? James Ciment claims that, "children in the United States today have more disposable income than ever before, with kids

---

[1] Andrew Zimbalist, Sherman, and Brown, *Comparing Economic Systems*. (San Diego: Harcourt College Publishers, 1988).
[2] Neil Howe and Strauss, *Millennials Rising*, 265.
[3] Lisa Eadicicco, "Americans Check Their Phones 8 Billion Times a Day." *Time* magazine, December 15, 2015 (http://time.com/4147614/smartphone-usage-us-2015/).
[4] Nicholas Carr, *The Shallows*, 116.

under 12 spending more than $20 billion a year and teens spending $155 billion."[5] How can the Church compete with this?

Consumerism is the idolized acquisition of more stuff. It is not a behavior, but a worldview and has become more pervasive than ever. The economy, technology, and cultural norms have created a serious challenge for the Church today. This challenge leads us to one of the most controversial ideas in modern-day ministry: that your church is a product to be marketed and sold to others.

Perspectives on the Seeker-Sensitive Church

The idea of making church more "seeker-sensitive" is not new. Some changes are good and include the switch from Latin to a common language, or bringing doughnuts. Other changes are bad, like pre-ordering indulgences or not bringing doughnuts.[6] Seriously, bring doughnuts.

For many years, America has had the corner on church-usability by launching a number of new denominations. In the early days, immigrants from Europe would expect to see a single and unified Church. In contrast, Americans would happily identify as Puritan, Congregationalist, Presbyterian, Episcopal, Baptist, Methodist, Universalist, Assemblies of God, or Church of God (not to be confused with Church of God in Christ).[7] It is impossible to generalize the motivations behind these church groups but we can safely say that the entrepreneurial nature of the New World helped foster this boom in theological branding.

---

[5] James Ciment, *Social Issues in America*, Volume 8:37.
[6] Edward Peters, *A Modern Guide to Indulgences*, 13.
[7] Craig D. Atwood,'*Handbook of Denominations in the United States*. (Nashville: Abingdon Press, 2010).

These denominations showed a renewed willingness to take the gospel to the streets and founded one of the most generous, socially aware, and charitable movements in the history of the world. An unprecedented number of hospitals, schools, and charities were birthed from these disparate Christian groups, many of which were more than willing to reinvent themselves in order to engage with the culture of the day.

The modern "seeker sensitive" movement has been designed to block church-histamines for those with a religion allergy. Leaders like Bill Hybels, Larry Osborne, and Rick Warren have been showing pastors how to draw a crowd and tell them about Jesus. Some leaders have followed suit by designing ministries for a non-Christian audience. Say goodbye to Sunday and Wednesday night services. Say hello to small groups.[8] But the question remains: Are all of these changes good? Have we traded *ministry* for *marketing* in an attempt to meet more people? And *where are* the doughnuts?

Your Church as a Product

We hate to think of our ministry as a product because it is not. Our churches don't make things, our brand has been the same for two thousand years, and our only upsell is to *love more deeply*. However, it is nearly impossible for people outside of your church to understand "ministry" in any other way. When they look at your church they see events, programs, and branding from a consumer's point of view. Stories from friends sound suspiciously like a multi-level-marketing and leave potential guests wondering, *what is the catch?* People want to know what they are buying before investing

---

[8] Also known as community groups, life groups, cell groups, fusion groups, mom groups, affinity groups, service groups, or that edgy group that meets in a bar.

time or money into your organization. Sometimes, the first way to judge a book is by its cover.

Your church must become influential within your community. This will require you to meet people where they are at. Some of the most uncomfortable places to go are the places that need Jesus the most. But what does it mean to go to where people are? Surely we are not expected to compete in the modern-day marketplace. Paul implored us to, "become all things to all people so that by all possible means [we] might save some."[9] Seriously Paul, *all possible means?*

Some churches have taken "cultural engagement" to the next level. Consider a Kentucky ministry that tempted new guests with a free steak dinner and chance to win a gun.[10] Other churches host Mixed Martial Arts fights and combat training for adults and children alike.[11] Who could forget Ed Young's *sexperiment* where he went to bed with his wife Lisa on the roof of his very own church?[12] These are a few examples of ministries going *all the way* to connect with members of the community.

Your church has been doing its best to become all things to all people. You may have multiple service styles, age-based ministries, and comfy seats. Do you want a cool name, website, or app? Sure you do. This is not a put-down of modern ministry; even your granddad wore "church clothes" to make a good impression on

---

[9] Zondervan, *NIV*, pt. 1 Corinthians 9:23.
[10] "Kentucky Baptist Church Gun Giveaway Draws People To 'Second Amendment Celebrations.'" *Huffington Post,* March 3, 2014 (http://www.huffingtonpost.com/2014/03/03/kentucky-baptist-church-gun-giveaway_n_4890017.html).
[11] A.B.C. News, "'Fight Church,' Christian Ministries Believe in Fight Clubs." ABC News, October 6, 2014. (http://abcnews.go.com/US/jesus-throw-punches-fight-church-christian-ministries-fight/story?id=25953786).
[12] See Ed and Lisa Young, Young and Young, "7 Days to Lasting Intimacy."at http://thesexperiment.com/about.

Sunday guests. I think that we would all agree that our church is not a product; but we still want people to buy in to what we are doing.

Responding to Consumerism

We are making progress here: the first step is to recognize that consumerism plays a dominant role in our society. The second step is to recognize that everyone lives in this society. Are you still with me? The third step is to help point these people to Jesus.

You can respond to consumerism in three different ways: reject it, accept it, or moderate it. The obvious answer is moderation but you must determine how to separate the good, neutral, and bad qualities of consumerism.

Moral Consumerism

Good aspects of consumerism might include a sort of *natural selection* process where only the best adapted and sustainable ministries continue on. For example: if people show up to the family movie night but skip out on the family polka night then you need to cancel the family polka night. (Besides, we all know that you shouldn't be dancing in church anyway.) In this simple scenario, the members of your church decide which ministry deserves to survive and which one needs to be ended.

I have personally begun several revolutionary ministry projects that were going to change the world. But when no one showed up for my revolution I was left high and dry. It turns out that my plans were not as good as I thought. People let me know by staying home that night and I had to eat all of the pudding myself. But that is a story for a different book. We all want to tell people about Jesus. So let's observe the behavior of others in order to determine which types of ministry can do the better job.

Another positive aspect would include targeting specific audiences. Larry Osborne is big on this and insists that effective ministry must take niche audiences into consideration.[13] His church pioneered the venue model where multiple styles of church are offered to the congregation at the same time, on the same campus. It is a sight to be seen. When you stand in the courtyard of their church, you are surrounded by different types of service options. It feels a bit like a food court. But this idea of niche marketing is a powerful one. Larry knows that many people feel uncomfortable in a traditional, or modern, church setting. These people are being reached by designing environments that appeal to their interests and needs. This aspect of moral consumerism is willing to, "bring the church to the people" instead of insisting that people come to the church.

Amoral Consumerism

Neutral aspects of consumerism would include ideas of branding and marketing. It's OK to brand your event, ministry, or sermon series. Cool graphics and logos don't necessarily impact the spiritual bearing of your ministry. That is, unless you create acronym-based posters for your "Worship, Teaching, and Friends" night.[14] Just because you look cool doesn't mean that you are selling out. Church leaders, throughout the New Testament, consistently adapted their methods to make the message of Christ ring more true.

---

[13] Larry "Innovation's Blind Spot: Is Protecting the Past as Important as Creating the Future?" (http://larryosbornelive.com/innovations-blind-spot/).
[14] Buckingham, "WTF Church." Michael Buckingham, "WTF Church." Church Marketing Sucks, September 6, 2010. (http://www.churchmarketingsucks.com/2010/09/wtf-church/).

Immoral Consumerism

Immoral aspects of consumerism lead to the selfish idolization of stuff. Even when the original intent of that stuff is to point to Jesus, human nature often places the shiny here-and-now before the everlasting Father.

Designing a ministry around the wants or desires of other people invites us to lose our focus on what really matters. The gospel of Matthew reminds us that you can only have one master.[15] Just ask the Village People about mission drift at the YMCA: showers, meals, hanging out with all the boys, and powerful altar calls... wait, one of those doesn't belong. The Young Men's Christian Association is not alone, many organizations were founded with a Jesus focus only to become distorted by popular demand. These include places like the University of Oxford and the Red Cross. However, the most dangerous consequence of leveraging consumerism in the Church is that of idolization. Many pastors and programs fall victim to this: people begin looking to them instead of looking directly at Jesus.

WHAT DO YOU DO?

The one thing we cannot do is ignore the role that consumerism plays in our society today. Christ has called us to share His good news with everyone. That means speaking Russian to Russians, Spanish to Spaniards, and Turkish to Turks. It also means that we need to address cultural differences within people groups. Jesus did this all the time when speaking to religious leaders, ethnic minorities, and foreign occupiers. His message was always the same but he chose different methods to address

---

[15] See Zondervan, *NIV*, pt. Matthew 6:24.

Pharisees, Samaritans, and Roman officers alike. If Jesus was willing to do it, then we can do it too. Don't reject consumerism outright. Timothy Keller observes that the countercultural approach to ministry can become pessimistic about social change, demonize modern society, and fail to give sufficient weight to the inevitability of gospel contextualization.[16] How are you going to respond the consumer-driven culture in our world today?

We need to know and be known by those who we want to reach. David Hesselgrave insists that modern missionaries "can effectively communicate to the people of any given culture only to the extent that they understand all aspects of that culture."[17] It is critical that you understand consumerism and learn how to respond to the good, the bad, and everything in between. Responding with moderation will require you to live "in the tension of being prophetic . . . while serving others and inviting them to a better way."[18]

Just remember that whatever you do, it's always important to bring doughnuts.

---

[16] Timothy Keller, *Center Church*, 207–8.
[17] Ralph Winter and Hawthorne, *Perspectives on the World Christian Movement*, 426. (Pasadena, Calif.: William Carey Library, 2014), p. 426.
[18] Gabe Lyons, *The Next Christians*, 173.

Reflection Questions

1. How has consumerism affected the way you promote your ministry to others?
2. What aspects of consumerism might help you minister more effectively?
3. How can you avoid negative aspects of consumerism that pose a risk to your current ministry strategy?

7.2 CHILDREN'S MINISTRY VERSUS CHILDCARE

Lauren Beach

"A person's a person, no matter how small."

Dr. Seuss[19]

While the words *childcare*, *babysitting*, and *daycare* bring delight to a mother's heart, they cause many children's pastors to cringe in frustration. Children's Ministry versus Childcare: it's a dreaded topic that makes me cringe whenever used to describe what is being offered for children during our weekend service. Don't people know that there is a big difference between a children's ministry and a babysitter? The truth is that many people don't have a clue that a difference exists. And does it really matter what we call it? Perhaps not. But we can all agree that it matters what we do. The heart

[19] *Horton Hears a Who*

behind your "program" matters and it matters that people understand what you are doing for the families of your church. It is important to establish a clear mission and vision for your children's ministries so that parents can clearly understand what is going on. It is impossible to equip parents as spiritual leaders if they do not understand what sort of spiritual foundation is being installed in the life of their child. In this chapter, we will begin the conversation about the difference between childcare and children's ministry, why it's important to distinguish between the two, and how to start a change in your church culture.

Coming to Terms

First things first: We need to define childcare and children's ministry. Childcare is a safe place for children to have their needs met and to be entertained and it is a safe place for children to experience Jesus. Second things second: We need to make note of two different but important venues. Children's ministry should intentionally partner with parents so that what children learn at church is the same as what they learn at home. In both places, children know they are safe and they are always loved for who they are. This is both simple and significant.

I have always felt strongly about effective ministry to kids; too many of our churches are content simply to keep kids busy. Jesus never commanded us to be busy; he commanded us to make disciples and this command does not only apply to people old enough to sit through an hour-long sermon. Jesus values kids and shows us that they are important. The family unit is the essence of the church and we must do whatever we can to nourish it and help it grow.

Your children's ministry is where children can discover who Jesus is and how much he loves them. Recall the passage from the gospel of Mark where parents were bringing their kids forward to be blessed by Jesus. The disciple didn't approve of this distraction and were keeping people from messing up Jesus' teaching schedule. But Jesus wanted the children to spend time him. It was important that they not be ignored or shooed away. I love how the New Living Translation puts it:

> But the disciples scolded the parents for bothering him. When Jesus saw what was happening, he was angry with his disciples. He said to them, "Let the children come to me. Don't stop them! For the Kingdom of God belongs to those who are like these children."[20]

It goes on to say that Jesus welcomed the children and blessed them.

Jesus showed us something very important, He showed us something that was very countercultural at that time: He showed us that kids matter. Jesus didn't want them to be overlooked or marginalized; he embraced them and blessed them. Jesus went so far as to tell his followers that "anyone who doesn't receive the kingdom of God like a little child will never enter it."[21] This verse isn't saying that we need to become children physically. It is telling us that there is something special about how kids view who God and that we should do the same.

Children understand that they need God, and they embrace him without holding anything back. They do this so well, and we as leaders have the chance to help facilitate this. Church is so much

---

[20] Tyndale, *Holy Bible*, pt. Mark 10:13-15.
[21] Ibid., pt. Mark 10:15.

more than a place for kids to go to get their physical needs met while the adults experience God's presence. We must be willing to create environments in which kids can listen and respond to the Holy Spirit. Children can understand God's mission and how each one of them gets to play a part, but we need to provide that opportunity. They view God in a pure way; they are not held back by the things that usually prohibit us as adults. Just think of the things they can do! Children of any age can experience Jesus, but we have to create an atmosphere where this can happen. "Children's ministries are helping set the foundations of faith that should be built on the gospel. We, as those who love Jesus and love our children, need to take this fact very seriously."[22] That is why children's ministry matters.

Why the Family Matters

How many of you have heard this conversation before? "Well isn't it all the same? Children's ministry, childcare, I don't really see a difference." Even worse, perhaps this question came from your lead pastor, a staff member, or from a parent. To most people, childcare means a place where you drop your child off, do whatever it is you want to do, then pick them back up. There may or may not be any relational component to this. The childcare provider sees that the needs of the child are met and enjoys the time with them, with no real need to get to know the families on a personal level.

As a children's ministry, however, we have a greater calling —to invest and support the family unit. The role of the Church is to build each other up, and to encourage one another (see Hebrews 10:25). Our role as children's leaders is not to just "watch" kids. We want to get to know each child personally and develop

[22] Powell, Clark, and Candy, *Sticky Faith*.

relationships with them. We need to show them that they matter to God and to us. That church is a safe place where they can come and experience a relationship with Jesus. But we also want to invest in families, and encourage parent to spiritually lead their children so that they can grow deeper with Jesus. Our job as children's leaders is to support and encourage families as we show them together what it means to have a relationship with Jesus.

Words Matter

When I first started at my church, I had to have the "childcare conversation" on nearly a weekly basis with parents, volunteers, and staff members. The posters printed for Easter announced that childcare would be provided at every service. I knew that most people viewed children's ministry as more than childcare, but it was frustrating to have to continually have the "childcare conversation" with our team. I had to realize that it was going to be a process, a process of communicating over and over again what the difference is.

While working through this at my church, I sat down with a children's pastor at another local church, and he communicated that change would not happen overnight and that it would to take time. He told me that in order to change the culture of my ministry, I would have to communicate the vision on a regular basis. One of the things he recommended was very basic: to remove the word "childcare" from the vocabulary of our children's ministry. That wouldn't mean we would stop offering what was once known as childcare, but rather that we would change what we called it. Now it would be called "ministry to kids." I discovered that the words I used truly matter, and people began to notice.

A few bumps came along with this change, but the families began to grasp the difference. During this process, a volunteer who is also a parent asked about our midweek childcare program. In that moment, I was able to communicate the difference between children's ministry and childcare and that conversation was the beginning of a cultural change. Through this conversation, I was able to spread the vision for children's ministry, and she walked away understanding our heart: that her children could come to know who Jesus is and that her family as a whole could be supported. When I overheard her explain the difference to another parent the next week, it was a win for me, a win for Jesus, and a win for children's ministry. This is what we want. If you are struggling in your current situation, be encouraged to know that even a small step is progress!

FLIPPING THE SWITCH

Understanding the difference between children's ministry and childcare should change how you communicate with the leaders around you. There is no one perfect way to do children's ministry; if there was, then we would all be uncreative and boring. And maybe some of the ideas I am presenting in this chapter will not work for you in your current church situation. That's OK! But I do encourage you to spend a moment thinking about the difference between the two, and about how you communicate the difference to your team and staff. Whether or not your church offers childcare, the thing that matters most is the heart and the mission behind the ministry. This can only be discovered when you, as a leader, spend time with Jesus. He will give you the vision and the means to make an everlasting impact in children's lives. At the end of the day, what matters most is that children are being introduced to a personal relationship with Jesus, and that families are being supported as they maneuver through the incredible task of leading their children's spiritual journeys. Doing that is what truly matters. Just don't call what you do childcare. What you and your team do is far more valuable than that.

Reflection Questions

1. How do you communicate the vision of your children's ministry?
2. How does your team differentiate between children's ministry and childcare?
3. What are three things you can do to establish a "children's ministry" culture in your church this month?

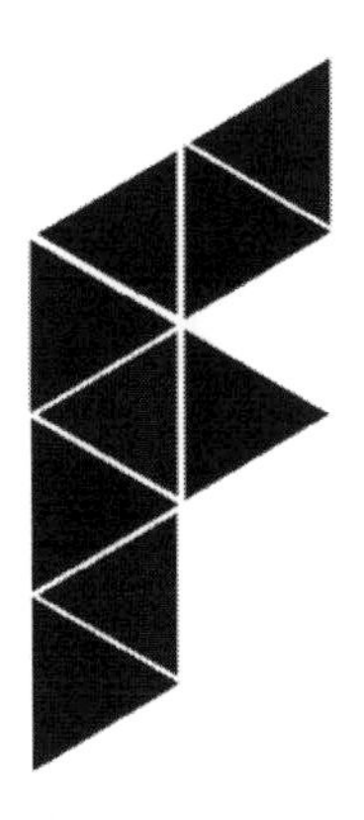

7.3 HARRY POTTER, IRON MAN, AND JESUS

Jace Murray

I can still remember the night we murdered Ariel, the little mermaid. Youth bonfires were a special summer tradition, with s'mores, Capture the Flag, and worship music blasting from a beat-up stereo, but this star-filled country night was different. This night, we had been asked to gather with a specific purpose in mind.

Our pastor had just finished a series on not being conformed to this world. In response, he told us that, in a giant communal ceremony of spiritual hygiene, we were going to purge our homes of anything secular that could dirty our holy status. Nothing was safe. Comic books, movies, cassette tapes, including any music that didn't have a high enough Jesus-per-minute ratio, were loaded into bags and brought to our puritan-bonfire. We were going to burn it all. To kick it off, our pastor was going to lead by example by bringing his preschool daughter's VHS copy of "The Little Mermaid" to use as tinder. I'm not sure if you were aware of this, but "The Little Mermaid" has a witch in it. Unacceptable.

My youth group's sin-burning party may surprise you, but I'm sure others are nodding their heads, thinking of similar memories of growing up in the Church. While I'm not suggesting that there were not things in our lives that need removal—what student doesn't have something he or she would be better off getting rid of?—I am not convinced that this was the most effective way to teach students how to engage the culture around them.

As leaders in children's ministry, we will have opportunities to communicate with parents and kids about their relationship with secular culture. TV shows, movies, music, books, games, and "screen time" are all things that many parents are concerned about as their kids get older and are introduced to the world they live in. How your children's ministry talks about popular culture is important because it shapes a spiritual worldview that can have a long-reaching impact, affecting how your students navigate their faith long after they leave your care.

How Big Is Your Bubble?

Everyone grows up in a bubble; it's just that some have bigger bubbles than others. Every parent protects their kids from certain things, and typically with great intentions. We're all familiar with parents who are culturally overprotective. I know of a well-meaning older church saint who would never eat deviled eggs because of potential spiritual consequences and encouraged others to do the same. We also know those who could benefit from introducing stronger boundaries for their families. (I'm talking to you, Mr. "My-six-year-old-loves-The-Walking-Dead.") There are, of course, many parents who fit somewhere between the two extremes.

Bubbles are often talked about negatively, but when you take the time to step back, it's easy to see the necessary role they play in our lives.

Whether you realize it or not, your children's ministry has a bubble too, and deciding how big that bubble should be is a huge part of setting the culture of your ministry. Some children's leaders view popular culture as a distraction and therefore completely reject it. They would tell you that we only have so many moments with children, and time is too valuable to allow anything other than Bible teaching to take place during a church service. On the other hand, some churches go overboard trying to fully embrace the cultural zeitgeist. They risk creating an environment that has the appeal, and spiritual depth, of a department store. Their worship songs include popular secular songs with lyrics adjusted to be about Jesus. By the way, hearing a room full of kids singing "Jesus, you're a firework" is an . . . *experience.*

Both of these types of churches have a great goal taken to an extreme. As children's ministry leaders, our primary goal is to teach the Bible to kids and to help connect them to the life-changing power of the gospel. One of the most effective ways of doing that is by helping kids relate to what they're learning. This is necessary so that your kids can internalize how it impacts their lives in very practical ways. Using stories, characters, and themes from popular culture is a powerful way to help kids to relate to your lessons. However, this certainly can be taken too far, and you have to find the proper balance in order to achieve the right effectiveness.

To start the process, take some time to write down your core theological pillars. These are the load-bearing supports which hold up the roof that creates your children's ministry; the framework your church culture flows within. Here is one of my pillars: I believe music has an incredible impact on how children view God. Because of this, I place a high value on the lyrics of the worship music we use. This drives us to prioritize songs which emphasize the character and nature of God over those that may be popular or otherwise great songs, but don't necessarily fit into our framework.

These decisions will rarely be easy. No matter where you draw the line—and a line must be drawn somewhere if you hope to form an identity that isn't ethereal—there will always be someone just on the other side of it who will want to know the reasons why you'll accept everything up to that point. They'll want an answer, and you need to have one. In the same vein, there will be some who may feel you have pushed that line too far. You also need to be able to explain why you allow certain cultural things into your children's ministry that some may not understand, or even disagree with. Knowing your "whys" is one of the most important core competencies of leadership and everything you do in ministry should be able to connect back to a "why." Start with your why, contextualize it to the culture and values of your church, and you'll find a great starting point for what cultural engagement in your children's ministry looks like.

The Confusion of Culture

It didn't take long after the release of the first Harry Potter novel for a vocal group of Christians to begin protesting it. Remember that? Where were you when *The Sorcerer's Stone* dropped? While libraries and teachers were praising the series for getting kids to start reading again, leaders of the Christian movement were accusing Harry Potter of teaching kids about witchcraft and the occult! I was a volunteer children's leader during the height of the books' popularity, and one day a student asked a really good question: "How come Harry Potter is evil, but *The Lord of the Rings* is OK? Don't both of them have magic used for good as well as for bad?" I didn't have a good answer for her.

The confusion of culture extends beyond the "why this, but not that" question. If a child grows up in a church context where popular culture is completely rejected, they run the risk of building a wall between their church life and home life. Some people call this the "secular and sacred divide." Over time this can encourage a person to behave differently inside and outside the church.

But teaching kids at a young age that it's OK to love Jesus as well as significant cultural elements in their lives such as Disney movies or Star Wars helps to build a holistic and well-balanced self-perspective within their spiritual worldview. They key here is consistency. We don't do for Jesus on Sunday what we are not willing to do the rest of the week. Likewise, we should not do the rest of the week what we are unwilling to do on Sunday. Finding ways to integrate our world experiences and culture with our Jesus experiences and culture is the very stuff that makes the gospel so powerful. Jesus should be an everyday part of our life and the Holy Spirit engages our hearts as we interact with the world around us.

Having now taken the time to read a few of the Harry Potter books as well as watch the movies (for research purposes only of course!) I discovered that the series opened doors to conversations with my kids about friendship, loss, sacrificial love, and a surprising amount of Christian allegory. Taking opportunities like this to show our children how their faith and Christian worldview is relevant when interacting with the culture, even (and especially) the popular culture, can become the training ground that prepares the young in faith to face the world outside the church door. Deciding which cultural landmarks to make use of as opportunities is the next step in establishing your children's ministry culture.

Reject, Receive, Redeem

A pastor once told me that we have three responses when interacting with specific points of culture. The first is to reject it. There is media content that my wife and I don't allow our daughters to watch. No surprise there. That's just called parenting. There are movies targeted for children that have themes we don't want to influence our kids, ranging from how kids show respect to adults to having content more mature than what we view as appropriate. There are also television shows so void of substance we have them on the no-fly list in our little corner of TV Land. (I'm looking at you, SpongeBob SquarePants). Similarly, as children's ministry leaders there are some elements of culture that we must reject and steer clear of in our children's ministry. Not everything that is popular in kid culture is redeemable. Churches may land on different perspectives for how they promote kids' events on Halloween, but I think we can all agree that we shouldn't show *South Park* clips in Sunday School.

The second option is to receive. There are many great things in culture that we can receive, especially when it comes to our environments. When we were remodeling our nursery space at church, one of the things I did was visit other childcare centers for ideas. They weren't Christian childcare centers, but they had some great ideas on room design, furniture, and age-appropriate toys. I live in Seattle. The Seahawks are a big deal here and Russell Wilson, the quarterback at the time of this writing, is very open in his faith in Christ. Our church hosts a Seahawks Sunday every year where everyone is encouraged to wear their fan gear. Part of that day is showing kids what it looks like to take advantage of being in the public spotlight to share the gospel of Jesus. This is an example of something in popular culture that we have received at our church; as we look at the world around us, we should be able to find many things that can be accepted into our children's ministry.

The third option is to redeem. Some things may not be designed with a gospel purpose, but can be used to influence others for Jesus. A few years ago we decided to have a "Superhero Sunday" as a bridge event to our "Trunk or Treat" (which can be another example of redeeming culture). There were a ton of Marvel Superhero movies coming out, and we figured a bunch of kids would have superhero costumes left over from Halloween, providing us the opportunity to invite them to dress up for a Sunday morning service. We decorated our kids' spaces to match the theme. For example, we designed our kids' stage to look like a hero's lair. We also had heroic music playing over our speakers as people entered the church, and all of the pastors wore T-shirts with their favorite superhero logos on them. Our kids at church were excited about the event and brought their friends, who joined many of the kids from our neighborhood we had invited at our Trunk or Treat event. After some themed games and energetic worship songs, we shared the story of how Jesus was the hero of our story and how he was calling us to be his sidekicks. The event was a huge success and brought a fun energy and sense of life that overflowed our kid's services and influenced the adult service. We used a similar strategy at our Easter egg hunt a few months later and themed it after medieval knights and princesses with a message of the Kingdom of God. When the day came, more than a few of our parents came dressed up, too, because they wanted to be a part of the fun of the event. It was contagious! When you find a way to tap into the fun part of popular culture that resonates in your church, and redeem it for the furthering of the message of Jesus, I think that you can find a surprising amount of success.

JESUS, CONTEXT, CULTURE

In the end, only you know what will work best at your church. Maybe you need to step out of your comfort zone and engage your kids where they're at in their culture. Some of you may have taken your acceptance of culture a little too far, and need to refocus on the essentials. Our primary role is to help kids find a saving relationship with Jesus and equip them to live a life of spiritual success. What that looks like depends on our context. What works in Seattle may not work in Chicago, and it will look different in Atlanta. Your context not only dictates your response to culture, it likely changes the actual culture that your kids are facing. As with any decision that dictates the direction of your ministry, it should be made prayerfully and in alignment with your church's mission.

Figure out which parts of the culture you need to reject: that which stands in opposition to the message of Jesus. Also find out what parts of culture you should receive. Our world is full of many wonderful and glorious things that speak truth into our world. Also consider which things are worthy of redemption. Many aspects of your culture are ready to be used as an illustration or reflection of the good news of Jesus Christ. Wherever you land on the spectrum, I think that we can all agree that Disney movies make terrible bonfire fuel.

Reflection Questions

1. How does your church decide when to engage with popular culture?
2. How do you keep Jesus as the primary emphasis of your children's ministry? Do any aspects of your ministry threaten to distract from the gospel?
3. What is a really cool event or special day you could do that redeems something culturally relevant to your kids?

PART EIGHT: PERSPECTIVES

The most important part of growing up is developing the ability to view things from the perspectives of others. This may sound like a simple and insignificant stage of human development but the transformation it enables is profoundly important. This vantage shift can take place between individuals or social groups. It asks the question, "how does this make *them* feel?" Or, *"what do they* want?" But let's not limit the embracing of different perspectives to the here and now. Viewing different perspectives may even transcend time. That's right Marty, it is possible for you to go back to the future and we want to take you there. Looking forward, and back, will help us see and understand the role of children's ministry more clearly.

Consider how you viewed the world as a young child; it was all about *you*. The desires and needs of other people were impossible to grasp. If you doubt this reality just spend some time with a two-year-old. They may be cute and sweet but they are definitive egomaniacs. Two-year-olds are oblivious to the needs of others and have only begun to master their own point of view. As they grow up, they begin to see other people and realize that these *others* have needs as well. Eventually, they determine appropriate times to put the needs of others first. This can only happen after children have been able to shift their perspective to the perspective of others.

This section will address issues of children's ministry over time. That is: past, present, and future. We will travel down the road of children's ministry from years past in order to more clearly assess where we are standing today. And after a quick refuel of the flux capacitor, we will travel to the future as well. As Dr. Brown once said,

"Roads? Where we are going we don't need roads."[23] Now quit looking at your mother like that and get going.

[23] Zemeckis, *Back to the Future*. Adventure sci-fi comedy directed by Robert Zemeckis, 1985.

8.1 CHILDREN'S MINISTRY OUTREACH AND EVENTS

Dan Metteer

I love to go to events. Fairs, parades, carnivals, festivals—if something fun is going on near me, I want to be there. I love making memories, and these kinds of diversions are the perfect way to do it. Judging from the number of other people that are usually in attendance at these events, it is safe to say that I am not alone. There is nothing quite like getting away to have fun with others.

I think God likes events too. Look at all of the feasts and celebrations that he organized in the Bible. There is the Feast of Trumpets, the Feast of Tabernacles, the Feast of First Fruits, the Passover Feast. All of these are big events that God did not just put together, but actually commanded the people of Israel to celebrate. Tons of food, unique traditions, big crowds—it sounds like a fun time.

When Jesus established the Church, he gave us a simple mandate to go and make disciples.[24] He didn't really talk about events. He didn't tell us we had to do a VBS or an Easter egg hunt, he didn't say anything about bring-a-friend prizes, and I am pretty sure the Bible doesn't mention trick-or-treats. But there is no doubt that Jesus created some memorable experiences for people. He turned water into wine at a wedding feast.[25] He miraculously fed thousands of people so they wouldn't have to leave the gathering to go home to eat.[26] And when Jesus calmed the storm, it was on a boat ride that it sounds like Jesus instigated just for fun.[27]

Why Do Outreach Events?

The simple answer to this question is: to invite people into the church community who would not typically come in for Sunday service. Does the Bible tell us to do outreach events? No. But we do have a mandate to go into all the world and make disciples. And if we are doing less than all we can to achieve that goal then we are lacking.

A few days ago, I had an eye-opening conversation. I was in the middle of a pre-marriage counseling session with a young couple that does not profess to have any kind of faith. They went to church a few times when they were kids—that was it. In fact, the only reason they even agreed to have a pastor officiate their wedding was as a favor to an uncle. They were a nice couple, but they really wanted nothing to do with God, Church, or organized religion. When the topic of parenting came up, I asked them what they would say when

---

[24] Zondervan, *NIV*, pt. Matthew 28:19.
[25] Ibid., pt. John 2.
[26] Ibid., pt. Matthew 14.
[27] Ibid., pt. Luke 8.:22–25

their child asked them questions about God. Their answer was clear and direct, "When we have children, we won't tell them what to believe. We think it is wrong to force that on someone. Whatever religion they decide to connect to, we will support." This couple went on to say that they had a relative whose religion was Norse mythology—he believed in Thor and Odin and Valhalla and all of the rest of this ancient folklore—and they supported his belief.

I left this meeting saddened about this couple and others like them as parents. How is it that this generation has bought into the idea that it is wrong to impress on their children what they should believe about right and wrong, about God and our relationship with him? But as I thought about this more, I realized that we, as the Church, have a unique opportunity in front of us. If the next generation of parents will not tell their children what to believe, but they will support them in what they decide on their own, then the opportunity is wide open to communicate the gospel to these kids.

The apostle Paul had this sentiment in mind when he wrote:

> But how can they call on him to save them unless they believe in him? And how can they believe in him if they have never heard about him? And how can they hear about him unless someone tells them? And how will anyone go and tell them without being sent? That is why the Scriptures say, "How beautiful are the feet of messengers who bring good news!"[28]

Over the past ten years, there has been an increased emphasis on family ministry (as opposed to isolated children's ministry), and in empowering the parent to be the primary spiritual leader in a child's life. This shift has brought an important balance to

---

[28] Tyndale, *Holy Bible*, pt. Romans 10:14-15.

the Church, and reminded us that the children's pastor must partner with moms and dads in order to see the most fruitful growth in kids. But we need to remember that our communities are bursting with kids whose parents have no awareness or desire, let alone ability, to foster spiritual growth in the lives of their children.

There will always be children whose parents cannot lead them spiritually. The church should support families. The church should equip parents to lead. But the church can never sit back and say, "OK, parents, lead your kids. We will be here if you need help." The church must remember that there will always be some cases where, spiritually speaking, the child will lead the parents.

I recently saw a video that illustrates the spread of the gospel throughout the world over the past 2000 years.[29] It is an inspiring look at how the message of Jesus has been steadily moving forward, spreading all over the globe since his death and resurrection. As I watched the video, I noticed something strange. There were a couple of points in history where a large portion of the world—all of Asia, for example—had apparently been reached with the gospel, but then the illustration showed that reach shrinking back and disappearing in a matter of fifty to one hundred years. I am no historian, and I don't know exactly what was happening during these periods, but it is a good reminder of this sobering truth: the Church is only one generation from extinction. If no new disciples are made, then Christianity will disappear from the earth in the next hundred years. I believe this will never happen, but I also believe that we are to preach the gospel as if it could.

---

[29] Isaac Botkin and Botkin, "The Spread of the Gospel Map." (http://westernconservatory.com/products/the-spread-of-the-gospel-map).

How Should We Do Outreach Events?

Be Intentional

This is the best place to start. It doesn't matter how many good ideas you have if they never actually happen. At the beginning of the year (or even six months out from the start of the year) sit down with your team, and plan out all of the events that you want to do over the course of the year—VBS, camp, holiday outreaches, special Sundays—everything. Then make note of when the planning for those events will begin. Make sure that your budget reflects what is going to be needed. And, finally, make sure others know about your plans—your pastor, your executive team, your church board, your church secretary—anyone who has influence at your church. Taking these steps will accomplish three things. First, it will allow everyone involved (including yourself) to get amped up over what is going to happen. It will allow everyone to look forward to what is coming up, and not let it get overshadowed by something else that gets put on the same weekend. Second, it will give you and your team the chance to be ready for the event. The bigger the event, the more time, preparation, and promotion will be required. And third, it will make you actually do it. It's tempting to want to cancel an event when the details become overwhelming, but when you put it on the calendar for everyone to see, you are more likely to tough it out and see it through.

Be Remarkable

There are many reasons why the percentage of Americans who attend church has dropped so dramatically over the past sixty-five years, but one of the primary reasons is this: People have so many more choices of other things they can do instead. If we are going to get families to come to our outreach events (or our Sunday gatherings, for that matter) then we need to make them *remarkable.*

Marketing expert Seth Godin says, "'Remarkable' simply means that a customer is willing to make a remark about it. If you can create remarkable products, people will talk about them."[30] In the church, we are not selling breakfast cereals or snow tires, but should we not be even more passionate than any business leader about making people aware that we exist?

And in this age of social media, people will definitely remark about remarkable things. In my town, football is huge. The week before the opening game, our children's ministry had our NFL team's mascot come and pose for photos with people at an outreach event that we held. Do you think people remarked about that? Absolutely! Facebook was filled with photos of moms, dads, kids, and babies who came to the event at our church and posed with "Blitz," the Seattle Seahawks' mascot.

The real remarkable story is the saving grace of Jesus. But, as Paul says, "How can they hear about him unless someone tells them?" A remarkable event can be the conduit that connects people to the Good News about Christ.

Be Relevant

Remember who these events are supposed to be for. There are a lot of events that churches do that are big fun for the insiders, but are not appealing to outsiders.

I worked with a church in an urban setting for several years. We hosted multiple outreach events at the church, but were never able to get more than ten or fifteen kids to show up despite how much effort we put in. So we decided that instead of inviting kids into

---

[30] Godin, *Free Prize Inside.*

the church building, we would go out into the community and host an event at a local park. Over 500 kids showed up! It was unbelievable the difference it made to get out of our building and into a public space. In that community, it was not a relevant idea to think that people would come into a church where they did not know anybody. We had to go to them. And one of the moms who brought her kids to that event ended up coming to the church, giving her life to Jesus, and later becoming the leader of the kids' church.

Why Outreach Events Work

Outreach events are not always easy to pull off. They can be expensive, they usually require a lot of volunteers to make them run, and they can take a toll on the leader. But before you let these reasons talk you out of doing events, consider these five reasons why outreach events work:

They give kids a reason to invite a friend. The first time I ever invited a friend to church was to an event. I was five years old. Our church had a special kid's speaker who came for three nights in a row. They said that if you brought a friend to church that both you and your friend would get a balloon. A balloon! That is all that this five-year-old little boy needed to get out there and do some inviting. I went to my neighbor's house and told him about the balloon. He was in.

I don't think I ever would have ever invited that neighbor to church on a regular Sunday. I would have been too scared. But the fact that it was a special day, and there was a remarkable prize (at least remarkable to a five-year-old) was enough to make the invitation easy. That is the power of an outreach event.

They aren't "church." As a dad, I get to see children's outreach events from a new vantage point. My daughters had some neighbor friends whose father was Jewish. He didn't have any religious practice happening in his life, but he had enough Jewish influence to make him unwilling to allow his kids to visit a Christian church. But one weekend at our church was "Rock Star Day." Kids got to dress like rock stars (spiky hair, sunglasses, Steven Tyler scarves—whatever) and they got prizes. The fact that this did not sound like church, combined with the fact that we had a Saturday night service, was enough to allow the dad to let his kids come with us.

People have preconceived notions about what we do at church, and many are negative. But outreach events can remove that stigma and open the door for invitation that might otherwise be closed.

They Get Talked About

In the same way outreach events can be "remarkable" by the families who come to them, they can also be remarkable to the influencers in your church. If you feel that the children's ministry at your church is generally ignored—banished to the basement—a successful outreach event (with some quality photos) can get your pastor singing the praises of children's ministry from the platform in "big church."

They Engage the Church

One thing that I both love and hate about outreach events is that they require a *lot* of volunteers. Volunteers are usually not easy to come by, but some of the best volunteers I have ever worked with in children's ministry began serving at an outreach event. The commitment level is low and the need is high, so many people will say yes to serving. Then they get to see what children's ministry is really all about, and the reward of seeing the positive impact on kids.

Some might start serving regularly in children's ministry. Others won't. But when we create opportunities for more people to get involved in ministry, it is a win!

They Become Part of Our Faith Story

Following my first few outreach events, I was disappointed that they did not make a bigger immediate impact on church attendance. I thought that if we had 200 new people come to a Halloween carnival on Friday night, that we should have at least twenty of those people come to church on Sunday. I was frustrated when that did not happen.

But later on, I started listening to the stories of people who did attend a weekend service for the first time. Over and over I would hear a story like this, "My kids came to your Halloween carnival. Then they came to your movie night, and your Easter egg hunt, and your VBS in the summer. Then the whole family came to your Christmas Eve service. We started to feel like we should start going to church, so here we are."

In the short term, outreach events don't seem to have a huge impact. But in the long term they can establish a relationship between the church and families in your community that is priceless.

Making It Happen

It is always difficult to add more to your calendar. Life is busy. But let that be an encouragement, not a hindrance. There will never be a better time to plan something creative, attractive, and impactful for the Kingdom of God than right now. Jesus has put you in leadership for a reason. Lead something great! You've got this.

REFLECTION QUESTIONS

1. What was one of your favorite events that you attended as a kid (church or otherwise)? Why did you go? What made it memorable?
2. What are five new event ideas that your community would find "remarkable?"
3. What events outreach events will your church do for kids in the next twelve months? When will they happen?

8.2 PENTECOSTAL CHILDREN'S MINISTRY

Dave M. Cameron

A single drop of water creates little impact, but thousands of drops falling one after another provide life-giving showers. Pentecostal children's ministry consists of thousands upon thousands of stories of people called by God to reach the next generation. Individual stories vary, with each leader using different techniques to reach children in their own unique ministry context. Some church programs gain national attention, while others remain local and serve a few children. Nevertheless, behind every story, people express a consistent motivation, namely, a desire to see children know Jesus.

A survey of the history of Pentecostal children's ministry unearths three common goals of individuals ministering to children. First, Pentecostals invested time to evangelize the next generation. Second, discipleship of children played a central role of many children's ministries within Pentecostalism. Finally, Pentecostals sought to minister to the physical needs of children.

PRE-PENTECOSTAL MOVEMENT

Pentecostal movements trace their roots back to the Methodist Holiness churches started by John Wesley.[31] This influence impacted other aspects of ministry such as the desire to see children grow in their faith.[32] William M. Wightman records the bishop's words in the Address of the Methodist Bishops to the General Methodist conference in 1850:

> [W]e must connect Methodism with whatever is true and valuable, pure and beautiful, in science and letters; and our children must identify the scriptural doctrines of the Church of their fathers with the recollections and associations, not only of the Sabbath-school room, but also in the halls of learning.[33]

The leaders of the Methodist Church identified the need to train the next generation as leaders not only in their churches, but also in their larger world.

Catechism and Vacation Bible School provided two ways in which.the Methodist churches sought to save and disciple children. Catechism played a role in training the next generation to understand the doctrines and beliefs of the church. John Wesley himself took the

---

[31] David Martin, *Pentecostalism.: The World Their Parish* (Malden, Mass.: Wiley-Blackwell, 2001).

[32] We could also consider the major influences on the life of John Wesley and their view of children's ministry in the Church. John Wesley was influenced by Count Zinzendorf and the Moravian Church. [See John Munsey Turner, *John Wesley* (Peterborough, U.K.: Epworth Press, 2002), 7-8.] Count Zinzendorf did not forget about children in his ministry with the Moravian church. He wrote hymnals for the church to sing, one of those hymnals appears to have been written specifically for children. [See "Prophetic History of the Moravian Falls Land and Mountain View Retreat Center," History: Moravian Falls, http://missionsbase.eaglemissions.org/history-moravian-falls/.] In addition to this historical fact, a cursory look at the present day Moravian Church shows an intentional investment in children through Sunday school classes, children's festivals, children's choirs, and more.

[33] William May Wightman, *Life of William Capers*, 360.

catechism he knew from Calvinism. Herbert McGonigle points out Wesley's familiarity with these catechisms: "It was the 'Shorter Catechism' that John Wesley gave most attention. Hidden away at the end of volume 14 of his 30 volumes, "A Christian Library," is his revision of this Catechism. He made no additions to it, but he did make some important changes."[34] John Wesley understood the value of catechism and included a catechism in one of his books.

In 1852, one group within the Methodist Church took another step in their use of catechism. William Capers, a bishop of the Methodist Episcopal Church, taught catechism for many years during his time as a local pastor.[35] Interestingly, just two years after the Methodist General Council in 1850, Capers published a catechism for children.[36] This work, entitled *Catechism for the Use of the Methodist Missions*, places a tremendous value on teaching and training children in the Methodist Church. Not only did Capers produce a full catechism for the purposes of missions, it appears the Methodist Episcopal Church commissioned their own catechism published in 1852, *The Catechism of the Methodist Episcopal Church.*[37] The observed goal of this work was to train young children in the ways of the Lord. The first picture in the book, under the word *"Catechism,"* displays a man sitting in a chair reading to a dozen or so grade school children who are standing around him, listening intently. Pictures appealing to a grade school age child continue

---

[34] John Wesley, *Wesley's Revision Of The Shorter Catechism - Primary Source Edition*, 59–63.
[35] Wightman, *Life of William Capers*, 247.
[36] This work is best viewed electronically as it has been scanned by Bethany Ronnberg and Jill Kuhn. "This work is property of the University of North Carolina at Chapel Hill. It may be used freely by individuals for research, teaching and personal use as long as this statement of availability is included in the text." The full work can be viewed here: http://docsouth.unc.edu/church/capers/capers.html. William Capers, *Catechism for the Use of the Methodist Missions Third Edition* (Charleston, SC: Published by John Early by the Order of the General Conference, 1853).
[37] Methodist Episcopal Church, *The Catechism Of The Methodist Episcopal Church*. (Whitefish, Mont.: Kessinger Publishing, LLC, 2010).

throughout the book. Clearly, this group took seriously the need to disciple young children in the "scriptural doctrines of the Church of their fathers."[38]

Vacation Bible School served as the second medium the Methodist Church employed to reach out to children. Barna Group research found that as recently as the summer of 2012, two out of every three churches in America host a VBS program each summer.[39] They have become synonymous with church summer plans throughout the country. Clint Jenkin states: "VBS remains a key way for churches to minister to their community—and not just to the kids, but to the parents as well."[40] Vacation Bible schools offer the ability for churches to engage their communities in a fun and meaningful way, thereby offering an opportunity for children to commit their life to Jesus.

Once again, the Methodist Episcopalian Church played a key role in the beginnings of vacation Bible school in America; they hosted the very first VBS. Steven Gertz writes:

> Unofficially, it's possible to trace the roots of VBS as far back as the 1870s, when the Methodist Episcopal Church offered summer Sunday school institutes. . . . In 1873, Bishop John H. Vincent proposed the movement should include educational and cultural programs, and soon other Christian groups across the country followed suit with their own summer retreats, many of them offering services for children.[41]

---

[38] "The State of Vacation Bible School." Barna Group, 2016 (https://www.barna.com/research/the-state-of-vacation-bible-school/).
[39] Ibid.
[40] Ibid.
[41] Steven Gertz, "From Beer to Bibles to VBS." ChristianityToday.com (http://www.christianitytoday.com/ct/2003/juneweb-only/6-30-43.0.html).

Again, a Bishop of the Methodist Episcopalian church did not hesitate to seize the opportunity to minister to children. The Methodist church's view of children's ministry served to inspire the new Pentecostal movement.

EARLY PENTECOSTALISM (1906–1950)

In 1906, God's Spirit fell on the Azusa Street Mission church in Los Angeles, California. William Seymour led the church. Cecil Robeck describes Seymour's intention:

> The Mission had a regular membership. It had a board of trustees. It incorporated. It bought and owned its property. It adopted a statement of faith, taking large parts of it from Parham. It ran a children's church on Sunday afternoons in the Upper Room on the second floor. On Monday mornings, it held what can be described as staff meetings or planning meetings for the work.[42]

In the midst of the miraculous healings, words of knowledge, and gifts of tongues, this local church did not forget the need to train up their children in righteousness. Every Sunday, at the center of what many consider the beginning of the outpouring of God's Spirit that led to what people currently know as Pentecostalism and the Charismatic renewal, the great spiritual outpouring at Azusa Street continued to hold Sunday School for children. Seymour never lost sight of the need to train the next generation of believers.

This desire continued into the beginning of the Assemblies of God. J. Roswell Flower served in the National office of the

---

[42] Cecil M. Robeck, "Azusa Street:100 Years Later" (http://enrichmentjournal.ag.org/200602/200602_026_Azusa.cfm).

Assemblies of God for many years as the movement began.[43] His wife, Alice Reynolds Flower, ministered in churches alongside J. Roswell during this time. She directed part of her ministry efforts toward children, writing Sunday school lessons as she served alongside her husband.[44]

The missionary endeavors of Marie Stephany and Gladys Hinson display an early desire to see children nurtured holistically early on in Assemblies of God history. Marie Stephany went to China in 1916 as a missionary and ministered to children.

During the great famine that swept across China in 1920 and 1921, parents who were unable to feed their children frequently sold their little boys. Many baby girls were drowned or left to perish in deserted fields. Moved with compassion, Marie shared her home with thirty of these unfortunate children. These were the first of many abandoned children who were brought to Marie.[45]

Stephany served in North China for twenty-six years, not only working with children but also planting several churches in the area. She also worked to see men released from their drug addictions and she lived long enough to see some of the orphans she raised become pastors and evangelists.

Gladys Hinson also attempted to respond to the call of God to go to China and open an orphanage in the late 1930s and early 1940s but World War II interrupted her plans. Undeterred from her ultimate mission, she opened an orphanage in Hot Springs, Arkansas with the blessing of the General Council of the Assemblies. Through her efforts, hundreds of boys and girls have received care

---

[43] Gary B. McGee, Self, and Wood, *People of the Spirit*. (Springfield, Mo.: Gospel Publishing House, 2014).
[44] Ibid., 197.
[45] Marie Stephany, "Mother Peace." Assemblies of God Heritage 17, no. 4 (1997): 36.

while hearing the gospel message in Hillcrest Children's Home, still in operation today.[46]

Marcus Grable earned the affectionate title of "Mr. Sunday School" as he served on the General Council from 1935–1949. The focus he brought to training teachers and encouraging everyone to join classes on Sunday mornings led to tremendous growth in the ministry. During his tenure as the national Sunday school leader, Sunday schools in the denomination grew by 300 percent.[47] He also sought to teach children the importance of supporting missions work as he launched the Boys and Girls Missionary Crusade (BGMC) near the end of his tenure. According to the history of BGMC, the Sunday School Department in 1949 recognized a need to teach children about missions: "If children are to grow up to be adults concerned about missions, then they must be taught about missions in their formative years."[48] Consequently, the Assemblies of God established a new children's missions education program—Boys and Girls Missionary Challenge (BGMC). The National Sunday School Department realized that "the not too distant future of our missionary work depends upon the vision of our children of this generation."[49] The program, adopted as the National Assemblies Missions program for children in 2001, proclaims a two-fold purpose as its mission: "to reach the children of the world," and "to create a heart of compassion in kids."[50] Grable and his team's vision proved effective and long-lasting as, to date, BGMC has raised over eighty million dollars toward missionary endeavors over the past seventy-plus years.[51]

---

[46] McGee, Self, and Wood, *People of the Spirit*, 218–19.
[47] Ibid., 287.
[48] "The History of BGMC" (http://bgmc.ag.org/about/history/).
[49] "The History of BGMC."
[50] Ibid.
[51] Ibid.

Marcus Grable stepped down from his position in 1949, but his support of Sunday schools never waned. He continued to serve in his local church to see children trained in righteousness. This service extended right up to the end of his life in 1970. McGee outlines a story just before his death:

> In retirement, his interest in Sunday Schools never flagged. Four days before his death in 1970, he participated in a parade that was part of a kid's crusade at Calvary Temple Assembly of God. Dressed as a farmer, he pushed a wheelbarrow on the three-mile parade route with a display he had made himself. The sign on it summed up his life's work: "Pushin' for Our Kids."[52]

The early years of the Assemblies of God demonstrated growth in many different ministries, including ministry to children. The desire to see kids saved, discipled, and prepared to preach the Good News of the gospel of Jesus Christ came out in many different ways through many different people.

Maturing Pentecostalism (1950–2000)

This commitment to see children saved and discipled through the Assemblies of God continued throughout the second half of the twentieth century. Building on the firm foundation established by Marcus Grable, the church designed two additional ministries to children with the purpose of seeing children grow in their Christian faith. The first ministry, officially launched in 1955, focused on girls maturing into women who knew and loved Jesus. This ministry actually dates back a little farther with the inauspicious beginnings of

---

[52] McGee, Self, and Wood, *People of the Spirit*, 288.

a single children's worker named Goldie Olson. Olson had a dream one night that lead her to create a missing link between children's church and youth programs. McGee tells her story:

> When Goldie Olson awoke from her dream, she realized God had provided the solution for reaching girls in the often overlooked "crack" between children's church and youth programs. In 1949, with this dream as her guide, Goldie worked with her pastor to organize the Cheerbringers club for girls. The program combined spiritual training (Bible reading and prayer) with more practical ministry to others (visiting local nursing homes and making handicrafts for distribution by missionaries to children in other countries).[53]

This program continued to grow and, in 1955, the National level of the Assemblies introduced it as a girls' ministry to allow older women an opportunity to train younger women in the faith in line with Paul's instruction in Titus 2:3–4.[54] The Missionettes program created a place where the older generation of women could mentor and equip the next generation through a badge-earning curriculum. Girls could earn badges through Bible reading, Scripture memorization, missions giving, learning life skills, and more. This ministry continues today as an effective part of ministry for women of God to train up young girls to become women of God.

The second ministry sought to train boys to become men of God. The Royal Rangers ministry began just seven years later, in

---

[53] Ibid., 565.
[54] "A Brief History of Mpact Girls Clubs | Mpact Girls Clubs." (http://mgc.ag.org/about/history/).

1962, under the leadership of Johnnie Barnes. It grew out of the vision of Burton W. Pierce. McGee outlines the need that Pierce observed in the 1950s:

> As the Assemblies of God experienced growth in 1950, Burton W. Pierce, then secretary of the Men's Fellowship Department, noticed a specific need: too many young boys were drifting away from the local church. Observing this disturbing phenomenon, he commented, "Our number one priority is to get men involved in soul winning and the discipling of boys."[55]

He empowered Johnnie Barnes to create a program for men to disciple young boys in the ways of God. Barnes created the Royal Ranger program. Similar to Missionettes, it also encourages boys to memorize Scripture, read the Bible, support missions, and learn new life skills through a badge-earning curriculum. Barnes' quote exemplifies the heart of the Royal Ranger program from both the need to serve and see boys grow in their faith: "A man never stands so tall as when he stoops to help a boy."[56]

In 1975, the institution of Junior Bible Quiz (JBQ) took place at the national level of the Assemblies of God. An offshoot of Teen Bible Quiz, the JBQ program challenges children to memorize 576 questions on biblical doctrine or Scripture memorization. This program resembles a Pentecostal catechism, teaching theology and doctrine in a question and answer fashion similar to what was done in the Methodist Episcopalian Church in 1852. The program successfully continues today.[57]

---

[55] McGee, Self, and Wood, *People of the Spirit*, 523.
[56] Gospel Publishing House, *Royal Rangers Leader Manual*, 193.
[57] McGee, Self, and Wood, *People of the Spirit*, 439.

In addition, this timeframe saw a rise of evangelism to children. These men and women toured the country with a ministry focused on seeing children come to know Jesus.

Paul ("Cowboy Smiley") and Myrtle Hild travelled about two million miles, conducting more than twelve thousand services while visiting 870 cities. Their ministry focused on children—kids' crusades. Child (preteen) evangelists such as Little David Walker, Uldine Utley, Mary Louise Paige, Charles Jaynes, and Dolores Lee Dudley also travelled widely, preaching in their own evangelistic campaigns.[58]

These ministers of the gospel did not forget about children in their evangelistic endeavors. In fact, they made the conversion of children one of their main goals as they travelled around preaching in the latter half of the twentieth century.

CONCLUSION

In Deuteronomy 6, Moses' address to the Israelites outlined the need to train the next generation. Pentecostals have taken this call seriously throughout their history. This brief survey of children's ministry clearly identifies three key characteristics of Pentecostal ministry to children. First, Pentecostal leaders have taken great efforts to evangelize children by introducing them to a relationship with Jesus through Sunday schools, Vacation Bible Schools, and traveling evangelists. Second, Pentecostals have invested abundant time and energy to see children discipled. Pentecostals saw great value in continuing what the Methodist Episcopalians started with their efforts in catechism, as observed through the Missionettes, Royal Rangers, and Junior Bible Quiz programs. Leaders like

---

[58] Ibid., 345–46.

Marcus Grable provided structure for programs that enabled children to flourish, changing countless lives in the process. Third, Pentecostals sought to effect change in the lives of children through holistic ministry. When they saw children with physical needs they sought to assist by bringing practical help along with the Good News of the gospel of Jesus Christ. Orphanages came to life through the hard work of women like Marie Stephany and Gladys Hinson.

Each story represented here tells only a portion of the overall story of the Assemblies of God throughout the years with regard to children's ministry. Countless stories will go untold for lack of space and knowledge. For sake of brevity and clarity, this chapter focused on the Assemblies of God, which represents but one shower of raindrops on this country. If every Pentecostal/Charismatic denominations' efforts were considered, a veritable deluge of showers would be observed bringing life-giving nourishment to everyone around.

Children's pastors and volunteers, take heart.[59] You stand among giants of the faith who have given their lives to minister to children.

---

[59] Zondervan, *NIV*, pt. Galatians 6:9.

Reflection Questions

1. How did the pre-Pentecostals contribute to modern day children's ministry?
2. What role should gender-based ministry play in your church today?
3. How can your ministry take cues from the early-Pentecostal movement and empower leaders to tell kids about Jesus?

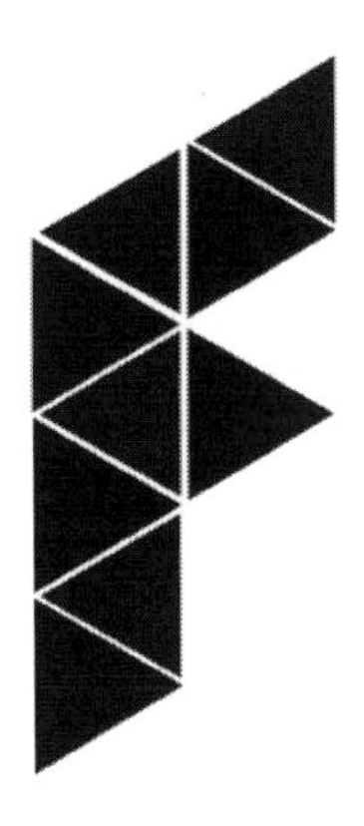

8.3 CHILDREN'S MINISTRY TRENDS

Bryan Reeder

When I was in elementary school (1977–1983) I attended an extremely traditional, fundamentalist, and conservative Baptist Church in Montana. I remember wearing my best clothes to Sunday school and singing songs such as, "Stop and Go," "Jesus Loves Me," and, "The Countdown Song." The song lyrics were on oversized poster board signs that kids held up. Like many churches in the 1980s, we met downstairs in the basement. After a while my parents stopped attending church but my brother and I rode the church bus for a few months on Sundays. The best part of riding the bus was the free candy we received each week. I loved the butterscotch hard candy and still love it today.

Looking back at my childhood experience in church, it's easy to recognize how so much has changed in children's ministry over the past forty years. In the past, children's facilities were sequestered and little thought was given to families moving from the parking lot to the classroom. Parents were expected to find the best ways to accommodate their children who might have learning disabilities. It was not unusual for children to sit right next to their parents on the church pew. Today, enormous effort is expended to guarantee that a family not only knows where the age-appropriate classrooms for kids are located, but that can also arrive there in five minutes or less—all while ensuring that it is the safest place in the entire church.

Today's kids— born from 2003 on—can be referred to as Generation Z. Their needs are different, they learn differently, and what they expect from your children's ministry is different. Seeking hidden generational trends is a notoriously frustrating proposition with a shifting and ever-changing culture.

A trend is simply a general direction in which something is developing or changing. Often in children's ministry we discover that the ministry we've created for one generation is outdated and ineffective for the next generation. The song, "Stop and Go" on a cardboard sign has lost its effectiveness with today's generation. As we seek the hidden trends, the clock continues to move and we are in danger of losing precious time in making a difference in kids' lives.

A Historical Perspective

Before I discuss potential future trends, it's important to grasp a historical perspective of children's ministry. As the old saying goes, "Those who cannot learn from history are doomed to repeat it."

The beginnings of children's ministry started with Sunday school as really the only trend. Sunday schools were originally literally schools; they were places where poor children could learn to read. The Sunday school movement began in Britain in the 1780s.

In America, the Industrial Revolution (1760–1840) resulted in many children spending all week long working in factories. Christian philanthropists wanted to free these children from a life of illiteracy. Since Saturday was part of the regular work week, Sunday was the only available time for these children to gain some education.

Therefore, the first Sunday schools in the United States were started in textile mills after the American Revolution around 1790. Samuel Slater, also known as the Father of the American Industrial Revolution, hired college students in Pawtucket, Rhode Island to teach children how to read and write in his own factories.[60]

The first national Sunday school effort began in 1824; its stated purpose was to organize, evangelize and civilize. Denominations and non-denominational organizations caught the vision and energetically began to create Sunday schools. Within decades, the movement had become extremely popular.

Mid 1800s

By around 1850, Sunday school attendance was a near-universal aspect of childhood. Even parents who did not regularly attend church themselves generally insisted that their children go to Sunday school. Working-class families were grateful for this opportunity to receive an education. They also looked forward to annual highlights such as prize days, parades, and picnics, which came to mark the calendars of their lives.

The focus was intentionally evangelical, and so within the next hundred years Sunday school had become the primary outreach arm of the church. The Sunday school organization now expanded to include all ages. Sunday school became a way for unbelievers to be introduced to, and then assimilated into, the life of the church. By the late 1800s, Sunday school was viewed as the

---

[60] Matt Guevara, "INCM—International Network of Children's Ministry" (http://incm.org/).

main hope for church growth, a view that continued until the mid-twentieth century.[61]

Early 1900s

According to Thom Rainer, the president and CEO of Lifeway, "By 1900 about 80% of all new church members in America first came to church through the Sunday school."[62] In 1902, Baptist minister E.Y. Mullins said, "Sunday School is the chief and almost only hope for church growth."[63] Reaching and assimilating people into the church was accomplished primarily through the Sunday school ministry. This trend continued until the mid-1900s.[64]

Late 1900s

As with all trends, the popular trend of Sunday school wouldn't last forever. During the late 1900s, Sunday school began to decline. In part this was due to the changes in child labor laws and the rise of the public school system. Children were no longer working six days a week. By the 1950s schools were open to children of all races. From 1973 to 1988 the Sunday school ministry "plunged 34 percent, from 40.5 million in 1970 to 26.6 million in 1986."[65] There are many reasons for this significant drop including the upsurge of teaching pastors, more churches growing to multiple services, and an ever-changing culture. During this same time period, evangelical Christians began reevaluating the way they were organizing church.

---

[61] Tanner, "A Brief History of Sunday School." (http://ministry-to-children.com/history-of-sunday-school/).

[62] Rainer, *Effective Evangelistic Churches*.

[63] Billy Nale, *The Sunday School as a Viable Tool for Church Growth in the 21st Century*. Liberty University, ProQuest Dissertations Publishing, 2007, dissertation number 3297908.

[64] Darren W. Thomas, "The Role, History, and Decline of Sunday School." 2005. Excerpt from dissertation at http://eridan.websrvcs.com/clientimages/36689/historyofthesundayschool.pdf.

[65] Ibid., 5.

The result was a trendy contemporary church movement which emphasized contemporary worship, relational small groups for adults, and experiential knowledge of the Lord.[66] The trend in children's programs was the rise of children's church which utilized more active-learning methods, while emphasizing "doing."

My first position as a children's pastor was from 1997–2001. Although we still provided Sunday school, children's church was developing for us as well. At time there was this conflict between traditional children's ministries and the movement toward a more contemporary approach.

Recent Trends

In the past twenty years, several trends have emerged in children's ministries. Trends are not always so positive. I certainly have never been accused of being a fashion trendsetter. Often the opposite is true. But some of the trends I see in fashion today don't seem positive to me. Not all of the following trends are completely positive. However, some trends have been constructive. Here is a list of ten of the more popular trends in the past twenty years.

Family Ministry

Although it's difficult to define family ministry. It is very unique from church to church. In essence, effective churches are finding ways to creatively challenge and engage parents in children's ministry. While church is important, God designed the family to be the primary place where discipleship happens. So the church's job is to come alongside families and help them fulfill the instructions given in Deuteronomy. In Deuteronomy 6:4–9 the Bible clearly teaches that

---

[66] Linda Weddle, "Trends in Children's Ministry." Kidzmatter.com, December 27, 2013 (http://kidzmatter.com/trends-in-childrens-ministry/).

parents are to train their children spiritually or to lead in the provision of spiritual development for their children:

> Hear, O Israel: The Lord our God, the Lord is One. Love the Lord your God with all your heart and with all your soul and with all your strength. These commandments that I give you today are to be upon your hearts. Impress them on your children. Talk about them when you sit at home and when you walk along the road, when you lie down and when you get up. Tie them as symbols on your hands and bind them on your foreheads. Write them on doorframes of your houses and on your gates.[67]

Safety First

Today's children's pastor is often a family counselor, savvy administrator, a staff manager, a bookkeeper, a pharmacist, as well as a lawyer and safety monitor. If your church has three to five core values for children's ministry, safety is most definitely one of those. Background checks and an application process to volunteer in children's ministry is now the norm. Many churches, including mine, now have security teams in place to emphasize the importance of safety.

Increased Technology

As in all areas of our culture, the use of technology in ministry is growing. Apps like Planning Center and connecting with families via social media are a great resource to children's pastors. The increase in technology certainly has its drawbacks. According to Pastor Jonathan Hansen of Passion City Church in Atlanta, "It's unsetting when churches remove the 'human factor' from worship. In

---

[67] Zondervan, *NIV*, pt. Deuteronomy 6:4-9.

other words, there seems to be a movement toward media-driven worship, even to the point that there are no people in front of kids."[68]

Our church recently responded to this increase in technology by having a camp called Unplugged in which we challenged our kids to turn down the distractions and turn up God's voice. It was an effective way to recognize the increase in technology and to challenge our kids on how that is impacting their lives.

Experience Required

Twenty years ago only large churches would have a children's pastor. Many churches are now hiring children's pastors as their second or third staff member. Smaller churches are often identifying the children's ministries team leader. Recently a church of less than forty people in my county hired a children's pastor. Churches are recognizing the need to have experienced, trained, and qualified individuals overseeing their children's ministry. Pastor Troy Jones of New Life Church says, "At New Life, our nursery and children's ministry impact everything we do."[69]

Changing Educational Methodology

This new generation prefers the interactivity of computer games, internet, and video games. Generation Z won't be content as passive observers. They want to use all their senses as they learn, and they want their learning environments to provide experiences, not just facts and formulas. Heidi Hensley, pastor at Bayside Church in Sacramento has her own concerns: "The negative trend I see the most is the need to take the Scriptures and form a drama that

---

[68] Weddle, "Trends in Children's Ministry."
[69] Troy H. Jones, *Recalibrate Your Church.: How Your Church Can Reach Its Full Kingdom Impact* (CreateSpace Independent Publishing Platform, 2016).

mentions nothing about the Bible and call it the lesson."[70] Some curriculums are leaning toward being more creative than they are Bible-based.

Conformity before Conviction

Generation Z is a highly loyal and personal generation. Because of this, they are (or will be) more likely to conform to their environment simply to fit in. They tend to be more open to other ideas. They are also loyal and prefer personal contact.

Changing Families

The "traditional" family structure is still in decline. Although the divorce rate hasn't changed much in recent years, your children's ministry may have as many non-traditional families as it has traditional families. New terminology is being created to describe the different types of family structures that you and I will come across. Families no longer rely on church to fill their social calendar. A family that is considered a regular attender at your church may only attend three out of every eight Sundays.

Pre-Teen Ministry

Ministries with the names such as "Club 56" are cropping up all over the nation. While the focus on tween ministry is a healthy trend, it is not as simple as treating preteen ministry as a mini or early youth ministry. This certainly looks different from church to church. You can emphasize a "Club 56" as a leadership team for children's ministries or you can focus on it being a transitional ministry between children's and youth's ministries. Whatever the

---

[70] Greg Baird, *The Future of Children's Ministry*. (online booklet) (Colorado Springs: KidMin360) (http://www.faithformationlearningexchange.net/uploads/5/2/4/6/5246709/the-future-of-childrens-ministry.pdf).

case, it is something to be considered as these kids are having experiences that used to be encountered at a much older age.

Relational Ministry

Children's ministries that are growing recognize the importance of relationship with the kids in the midst of their programming. In the 1980s and 1990s there was an emphasis on entertaining kids as children's churches grew and Sunday school declined. Bigger was always better. Even with the decline of Sunday school, today the value of small groups and relationships is emerging. Through relationships children can be greatly impacted and then changed.

Special Needs

One encouraging trend is that many churches are moving away from cookie-cutter approaches to ministering to children, and that includes acknowledging that many kids come with special needs that need individual focused attention. One out of eight-eight children has an autism spectrum disorder; 10 percent of children have an anxiety disorder; 7 percent of children have ADHD; and 8 percent of children have a learning disability.[71] In my experience this is a great opportunity to reach a group of people that are fairly unreached.

Future Trends

What is the future of children's ministry? What are the future trends? In my twenty years as a children's pastor, I can look back and point to programs, events, and resources that I simply don't use anymore. Puppet shows, flannelgraphs, film strip shows, VCRs,

---

[71] Amy Fenton Lee, "The Inclusive Church." Leading a Special Needs Ministry Book to Be Available Again" (https://theinclusivechurch.wordpress.com/).

Nintendo GameCube, chalkboards, vests for our student leaders, worship via cassette players, Kids Crusades, overhead projectors, human videos, VeggieTales, Bible Man, Train Depot children's church curriculum, monthly newsletters that were mailed, and even glitter. Glitter is way too messy. Methods change from generation to generation, and we must be ready to adapt so that we can connect to today's kids.

In answering the question "What is the future of children's ministry?" Karl Bastian says, "I'm always faced with a very real dilemma. Do I respond with my Predicted Future, or my Preferred Future?"[72] What I want, what you want, may not actually happen. It may not even be the best for the future of children's ministry. I love change when I'm the person initiating change. But when I'm not, it takes me a while to process change and get on board.

The bottom line is that the future is going to be different than today. As trends evolve, we as leaders must adapt so that we can connect and reach the next generation. Children's pastors and churches will need to continue to rethink programs and methods in order to consider how best to address the needs of the current culture. I foresee the following trends to continue or to burst upon the scene.

Local Curriculum Development

Fewer traditional curriculum companies will exist; therefore, the best curriculum will be from churches. Curriculum companies are already dying or are merging with others. Many of the effective resources today are from churches producing and using those resources. I'm confident that this trend will continue.

---

[72] Baird.

Church Online

I have no idea how this will look or if even this is an advantageous trend. Recently I heard about a child who was sick at home, but through Facetime she could experience Kids Church live without being present. Future leaders will think outside the box to leverage technology for the greater good.

Special Needs Ministry

Today we know so more about special needs children than we did even ten years ago. With increased knowledge we will be able to develop ministries to reach this often-unreached segment of our population.

Relational Ministry

One key to connecting with Generation Z and future generation will be relational discipleship. A growth in mentoring and coaching relationships will emerge in churches.

Live, Interactive Worship

This is one of those trends that shows up in my preferred future. My hope is that leading kids in worship with live bands will be a trend in many churches instead of the minority of them. It's easy to lean too much on YouTube videos and technology. Live, interactive worship gives children opportunities to experience God in a life-changing way.

Family Ministry Over Children's Ministry

Emphasizing parental influence and partnering church with the family will be an underlined trend. Family pastors will have greater influence in the local church than ever before.

Rick Chromey says:

> Ultimately, the cultural signs point to children's ministry becoming more home-based, experiential, virtual and networked. Consequently, a new type of leader is needed. Someone who thinks without boxes, embraces circles not squares, leads from the edge not the middle and employs digital frames as relevant cultural bridges.[73]

Closing Summary

Today it's about Generation Z, but soon a new generation will arrive. In just a few years, Generation Z will be our parents in children's ministry. We used to worship in children's church with cassette tapes or with no music at all! Then came CDs and now it's YouTube videos or live bands. Something new is imminent.

Read everything you can about upcoming trends, immerse yourself in studying kid culture, and have the courage to implement what you learn. And as we implement these new ideas, we need to keep in mind the "why" behind these changes. It's about getting hold of a child's heart and showing them how much God loves them. It's about reaching their soul and having them see Jesus in a way that is relevant to them.

Michael Chanley says,

> We can't know what the future of children's ministry or the future of anything else will bring. However, let me urge you to make your best efforts to prepare for tomorrow by living for today. Do not become complacent and accept the status quo. Make a difference. Fight to advance the gospel message.[74]

---

[73] Baird, *The Future of Children's Ministry*.
[74] Ibid.

Generation Z and future generation need pastors, leaders, and churches who will think outside the box, who will take risks, who will challenge the status the quo, who will lead courageously, and who will be faithful in spreading the gospel accurately in a way that connects to their current culture and generation. Will you be one of those?

Reflection Questions

1. What can you learn from past trends?
2. How will your children's ministry look different ten years from now?What courageous decision can you make right now to better connect to Generation Z?
3. What do we do with today's pre-teens?

PART NINE: PASTORAL MINISTRY

Our final section explores pastoral ministry in the local church. We understand that the role of a pastor is to look after and lead members of the congregation. This care is often expressed through counseling, coaching, and providing general support. The word pastor is akin to the caretaking of livestock and the Bible is full of shepherding metaphors. Old Testament heroes like Abraham and David cared for sheep; and Jesus loved a great sheep metaphor to get things going. Most of us understand the idea of shepherding and how the metaphor relates to the type of care and attention that a pastor gives to his or her congregation.

But what does it look like to pastor children? Relationships with kids are much different from relationships with adults. Is it possible to offer guidance and insight to entire families who are experiencing grief or trauma? And how can we support our pastor as they lead the church? This final part of the *Fusion: Children's Ministry* series will tackle these questions and more.

Remember, just because people don't call you pastor doesn't mean that you can't care for them as a pastor does. Some churches hold this title dearly and won't just allow anyone to use it. Our use of the word pastor and pastor refers to the methods by which we care for those who have been entrusted to us.

9.1 SPIRITUAL PARENTING PRINCIPLES

Nick Caalim

How many times a month do you see the same child in your weekend ministry? Three times a month? Three times a quarter? Certainly there are those who attend regularly—I like to call these my 52-weekers—but they are few and far between. These are the kids whose names you know. You have a relationship with them and know what makes them laugh and how to engage them in conversation. You likely know their parents' names too, and where those parents sit in the adult service. Aren't you grateful for these kids? You know your ministry is making an impact on their lives as you've seen the spiritual fruit and their knowledge of God's Word grow. Take a minute to thank Jesus for the special bond you have with these families. Say their individual names. Go ahead, we can wait.

After this super-consistent group, you probably have those kids who show up two or three times out of the month. And just like the group mentioned before, these kids probably try to skip your check-in process too. And, just like before, the bond you have share with these families is special and unique. Treasure your role in their spiritual development.

There are others that show up too. You've got those kids whose faces you kind of know, and if you've been in ministry at your place for a while you might be able to recall their name with some help or prompting. I'd imagine this is the crew that needs frequent reminder of the "R.U.L.E.S." for the class. But the good thing is your jokes are still new to them! Your weekend ministry is still a novelty to these kids and you get plenty of opportunities to wow them with props, games, and buckets full of candy.

Regardless of how often you see these kids come through your door, one thing is true: Each represents a great opportunity. And another thing is true: You, as the children's pastor, leader, director, or teacher are not the most influential person in their life when it comes to their spiritual growth.

Sorry. I'm sure this is not new news to you. As an experienced children's ministry leader you understand that the children's ministry and its leadership can never take the place of primary spiritual influencer in a child's life. That role has been, and always will be, the child's parent or direct guardian. Keep in mind that these men and women are the primary influencer in both positive ways (which leads to following Jesus), and negative ways (which prevents following Jesus, or places no emphasis on Jesus whatsoever). There have been many books and trainings about this concept which I am sure you are familiar with. We won't go into the depths of this topic in this reading; take a closer look at some of the sources cited in this book for further reading.

This reading will focus on how we can provide a framework for parents to maximize their spiritual influence over their children. No matter how often a family walks through the doors of your church building, you can energize the children to want to seek after Jesus and equip parents to engage their kids in spiritual growth. The rest of this reading will focus on five guiding principles to help parents maximize their influence.

However before going any further it would be good to point out that what you are about to read isn't a list of to-dos or very specific activities to put into action. Rather, these are principles that can help guide action. Principles are like a road; your car has the opportunity to change lanes and you can course-correct as needed (unlike a train track, where you can't do anything but go forward and back).

Spiritual Parenting Principles

Principle 1: Authentic Faith

Your children are looking for something real and alive, and the first place they are going to look is you. Successful spiritual parenting starts with the authentic faith of the parent. Think of it like this: Would you ever by a Dodge from a car salesman who refuses to drive nothing but a Ford? It is a lot harder to instill faith in your kids when it is not something you have wholly bought into yourself. And when we say faith, we are not talking about a religious set of rules to follow, but a vibrant relationship with Jesus. Faith must become more than a compartment of life, like work, school, and hobbies; it must become integrated into our whole life.

Faith is not passed down biologically. Just because a child has your DNA does not mean that your faith is automatically transferred. A child learns from what they see and experience. A child's faith will grow from the faith they see and experience in you.

> Hear, O Israel: The Lord our God, the Lord is one. Love the Lord your God with all your heart and with all your soul and with all your strength. These commandments that I give you today are to be on your hearts. Impress them on your children. Talk about them when you sit at home and when you walk along the road, when you lie down and when you get up. Tie them as symbols on your hands and bind them on your foreheads. Write them on the doorframes of your houses and on your gates.[75]

Principle 2: Attentive

The day-to-day life of a parent can become consumed with both routine and managing chaos. Most days, success is defined by just getting everyone out of the door. Managing schedules and accomplishing tasks are necessary but only scratch the surface; a spiritual parent must step back to assess the spiritual climate of the household. Imagine yourself as a spiritual thermometer, with the ability to gauge the spiritual health of your family. "Do I see any spiritual fruit in my children?" "Is God doing anything in my kids?" "Is our family spiritually alive at home?"[76] A spiritually attentive parent must take the time to ask and honestly answer questions like these.

In addition to the need for attentiveness to the family as a whole as mentioned above, there must be attentiveness that is focused individually. Listening to your children and asking them specific, open-ended questions are great ways to evaluate what God

---

[75] Zondervan, *NIV*, pt. Deuteronomy 4:6-9.
[76] See Ibid., pt. Galatians 5:22.

is personally doing in their lives. This opens the door for you to spiritually engage with your kids. You can also look for emotional trends.

Keep in mind the principle is about being attentive, which is not necessarily the same as being a detective. What's the difference? Attentiveness means being close enough to pick up on the nuances of how your children are spiritually reacting to the challenges and joys of life.

Principle 3: Leadership

If you want your kids to learn how to swim, you take them to swim lessons. If you want your kids to become more active, you take them to soccer practice. If you want your kids to love and follow Jesus, you take them to church, right? No. The church is not the primary spiritual influence for your children—you are. A spiritual parent is one who has taken responsibility for his/her children's spiritual health. Just like a thermostat, the parent sets the temperature or the spiritual climate of the house. The parent is directly and primarily responsible for connecting his or her children with Jesus. But don't freak out. Being a spiritual giant is not required. A parent is leading spiritually when:

1. Jesus becomes a priority in the family.
2. Jesus is welcome at the dinner table, in common life.
3. He or she engages children in spiritual life.

Spiritual parenting does not require you to be a perfect parent. But it does require you to allow the Holy Spirit to lead you as you lead your children towards his kingdom. Consider these words from Michelle Anthony, "I parent in a way that does not simply spend my hours but allows me to invest my days toward eternity."[77] Paul commended first generation Christians in the city of Corinth: "Follow me as I follow Christ."[78] And Joshua, leader of the people of Israel, proclaimed, "as for me and my household, we will serve the Lord."[79]

Principle 4: Discipline

Spiritual parenting is not about raising children with all the right behaviors. It is about nurturing in them a love for Jesus. As parents, especially Jesus-following parents, we place an emphasis on our children's behavior. We check to see if our kids are doing all the right things, but do we check the condition of their hearts? A child must understand that faith is not just knowing all the rules, but knowing Jesus first. The solution is not behavior modification, but heart transformation. Keep it simple. A spiritual parent instills within his or her children disciplines that will keep their faith vibrant—like prayer, Bible reading and memorization.

> Blessed is the one
>   who does not walk in step with the wicked
> or stand in the way that sinners take
>   or sit in the company of mockers,
> but whose delight is in the law of the Lord,
>   and who meditates on his law day and night.
> That person is like a tree planted by streams of water,
>   which yields its fruit in season
> and whose leaf does not wither—
>   whatever they do prospers.[80]

---

[77] Michelle Anthony, *Spiritual Parenting.: An Awakening for Today's Families* (Colorado Springs: David C. Cook, 2010).
[78] See Zondervan, *NIV*, pt. 1 Corinthians 11.1..
[79] Ibid., pt. Joshua 24:15., NIV
[80] Ibid., pt. Psalms 1:1-3., NIV

Spiritual disciplines help make this scripture passage, and the promises it contains, a reality for our children. A spiritual parent makes these disciplines a priority.

Principle 5: Speak Truth

Throughout the day, your children will encounter any number of opinions that demand their attention and try to tell them who they are. Parents can address these voices from the world in one of three ways. They can isolate, insulate, or ignore it altogether.

Likely the most common approach is to ignore the influence of the numerous opinions out there. In this passive approach, you actually validate and give equal weight to every voice, including your own. Then when a tough choice needs to be made, the route your child picks will be the loudest, the one that "feels right," or the opinion they heard most recently. Ignoring the fact that there are multiple voices of opinion for your kids to listen to creates numerous options, seemingly all equally valid, when in reality your voice ought to trump them all.

Isolation aims to protect children from evil influences through completely sheltering them from the world. This has its place in parenting, but only to a certain point. Once the protection of isolation is gone, the world is still ready and waiting to take full advantage of their curiosity.

Insulation, however, prepares the hearts and minds of children to interpret the world around them. Spiritual parenting takes a proactive stance to speak the truth of God's word into the hearts and minds of their children. This then provides a foundation for children to filter the countless opinions around them. Consider the importance of having properly installed insulation for your home. It is a part of the home that has profound impact on the sustainability of the home during both harsh winters and severe heat of summer. To maintain consistency within the home, the key factor is the insulation surrounding it. Insulating your child's heart and soul has a similar effect as your kids go through trials in their lives. Your words provide such insulation.

Do not underestimate the power of your words to instill within your children their value as children of God. They have the influence to change the world around them right now! And as a spiritual parent, it is your role to speak this value into their lives.

The principles of authentic faith, attentiveness, leadership, discipline, and speaking truth are powerful tools for parents to use to help guide them in spiritual parenting. Regardless of your age or tenure within your ministry you can be a source of inspiration and encouragement to the parents in your church. Keep in mind, you offer guidance on spiritual growth and not necessarily on child development, behavior issues, or even general parenting. If you can offer insight on those things, by all means, do it! But don't forsake your discernment on matters of spiritual development. You are in position as the expert for children's spiritual growth. So maximize your impact and influence to in that direction. The parents within your ministry need to rely on you for inspiration and encouragement to become the best spiritual leading parents they can be.

Reflection Questions

1. How can you help parents promote authentic faith in your children's ministry?
2. What does it look like to model attentiveness in your own life?
3. What are three things you can do this month to engage parents with the teaching of your weekend ministry?

9.2 A HOW-TO GUIDE FOR SPIRITUAL FORMATION

Dorene Heeter

One of the main goals of children's ministries is to strategically partner with parents in the spiritual formation of their children. Let's take a moment and define the term, "spiritual formation." *Spiritual formation* is a lifelong process of becoming a disciple of Jesus by learning how to become more like Him. But what are the measurable moments that define this growth process and how can we ensure that the children we minister to are making progress in their spiritual journeys? Let's take a closer look the parents' responsibility and examine how we can provide tools to encourage spiritual growth.

We see in Scripture where God addresses parents and commands them in this way,

> The Lord your God has directed me to teach you his commands, rules, and laws. Obey them . . . then you, your children and their children after them will honor

the Lord your God as long as you live. Obey all his rules and commands I'm giving you. If you do, you will enjoy long life. Israel, listen to me. Make sure you obey me. Then things will go well with you. That's what the Lord, the God of your parents, promised you.

Listen to me. The Lord is our God. The Lord is the one and only God. Love the Lord your God with all your heart and with all your soul. Love him with all your strength. The commandments I give you today must be in your hearts. Make sure your children learn them. Talk about them when you are at home. Talk about them when you walk along the road. Speak about them when you go to bed. And speak about them when you get up. Write them down and tie them on your hands as a reminder. Also tie them on your foreheads. Write them on the doorframes of your houses. Also write them on your gates.[81]

Since the spiritual foundation of a child's life is usually formed at a young age, the home is the front line of introducing and training children in their God-journey. The responsibility rests first and foremost on the parents. And the church is to partner with and assist parents to help train children to know and love Jesus by providing the best kids' ministries and resources we can. Our goal is to guide families as they grow in their relationships with Jesus.

This task of partnering with parents can be challenging for the children's pastor or leader. In a rushed world filled with overloaded schedules and an on-the-go mentality, parents often see kids' ministries as babysitting or at best, a place their child will

---

[81] Deuteronomy 6:1–11, NIV

receive the only spiritual instruction they will need. Teaching parents to take the spiritual lead is often hard and a challenge I have discussed with other leaders. I have even experienced it when we've provide classes or training for parents and so few attend or take action to implement the tools given.

As a result, our children's leadership team gathered some faith-coaching skills and broke them down into bite-size chunks that parents can assimilate into their daily lives. Instead of one long meeting or a series of class sessions, we experimented with quarterly parent orientations called *Parent Previews*. We then outlined these simple faith-building activities that could help parents lead their children spiritually and see their kids grow strong in their faith all throughout their childhood. Here is a list of some of those activities.

Faith-Building Activities with Kids

Devotions: Bible Reading and Prayer

Encourage parents to invest in a great children's devotional book, give recommendations and provide a list on a children's ministries resource page within your church's website or social media.

Encourage parents to pray daily with and for their children. Provide simple monthly guides or tools that set parents up for success to accomplish prayer times.

Encourage parents to memorize one verse together as a family each week. Link the Scripture verse to current lesson plan of Sunday morning. Provide a take-home parent guide to "what's next" in the teaching series of your kids' church or class, allowing parents to be "in the know" so that they can have meaningful conversations about the lesson and offer memorization help for the verse(s).

Encourage parents to read Scripture together. It doesn't have to be much, but it has to be clear that God's Word is an important resource and part of daily life. Kids need to see their parents reading their Bibles and praying —this is a spiritual formation lesson that is both caught and taught. Provide parents with a list of Bible suggestions they could purchase for their child.

Teachable Moments

Help parents see the need to *be* with their children daily by talking, listening, and applying Bible truths to life: These are the things that happen in the parents' lives and that happen in the kids' lives. God wants to be a part of every aspect and situation that comes their way.

Father and son, pastors Hugh and Brad Rosenberg share a passion for prioritizing the raising of the next generation.[82] They use the acronym LEAD THEM as a summary of their advice on the subject of helping parents to lead their children spiritually. It can be an easy tool to guide parents:[83]

Love them. Every child and every person on the planet needs to feel loved. You can demonstrate love by spending time with your children. What if you decided to make an impact right where you are?

Train them. Train your children not just how to do the things you know how to do, but teach your children your spiritual beliefs and why you believe them. They

---

[82] Hugh Rosenberg and Rosenberg, "Father Print." (http://fatherprint.com/).
[83] Hugh Rosenberg, "Lead Your Children." Pentecostal Evangel, June 17, 2012. (http://tinyurl.com/zfbgnqe).

learn more from your actions than they do from your words.

Have fun with them. Learn how to play and joke around with your children. They need to learn how to relax and unwind from the stresses that they have in their lives. Make it a goal to make memories.

Equip them. Help your children understand what they are good at and provide them guidance in how they can develop their strengths.

Motivate them. Teach your children how to set goals and reward them when they accomplish those goals. If your children are rewarded for good behavior, then they will be inclined to repeat that behavior.

Celebrate Spiritual Milestones:

Provide opportunities and tools to celebrate spiritual milestones in kids' lives. We have created and provided award-type certificates as a visual reminder of kids' spiritual growth. Parents from our church have scrapbooked, framed, and even spiral-bound into a book these simple certificates as a way to celebrate their child's spiritual development. We provide these "Milestone Certificates" (as we like to call them at our church) at each of the Kid Check-In stations, which serves two purposes—as a reminder to the parents and as an easy location to pick one up. You can even choose to leave a signature line for a pastor or children's leader to sign once the parents have filled it out. Often parents put on display their child's artwork, trophies, and awards, to celebrate their child's successes, however, most parents do not have a tangible or visible way to celebrate spiritual growth; those important milestones of their faith.

Let's provide parents with memorable and simple ways to celebrate those spiritual milestones in their child's lives. We want our parents to discover that, "I have no greater joy than to hear that my children walk in truth."[84]

Milestones to be Celebrated

When we decided as a children's leadership team to help our parents celebrate the spiritual milestones of their kids, we brainstormed and fine-tuned a list for parents to utilize. This was a great tool for our parents and a great tool for our children's staff to be able to rally behind and encourage parents. We became even better cheerleaders of the parents, encouraging them in every growth stage of their kids! Here is our list. It is not exhaustive and we may have missed a few, but I hope it will get some ideas flowing as you create a list of wins in a child's spiritual life. This is a great tool for your children's team to encourage parents as they strive to be the spiritual leaders of their kids. They can do it!

Here is a list of some of the ways Milestone Certificates can be given for each childhood time period:

Baby Dedication

Scripture: "He took the children in his arms, placed his hands on them and blessed them" (Mark 10:16, NIV).

Moment: After attending a class and dedicating a child, receiving a pastoral and church blessings and prayer during a service.

---

[84] Zondervan, *NIV*, pt. III John 1:4., NIV

Nursery (Infant – 2 Years)

Scripture: ". . . receive the kingdom of God like a little child. . ." (Mark 10:15, NIV).

Moment: To introduce young children to a loving, nurturing and positive first church experience, each family receives a welcome packet, blessings booklet, and "Baby Blessings Bible" that includes praise, Bible stories, monthly blessings, and prayer.

Develop: Daily Bible reading and prayer at home that builds faith. (Suggestion: incorporate into your night-time routine.)

Early Childhood (3 Years–Pre-K)

Scripture: "'What then is this child going to be?' For the Lord's hand was with him" (Luke 1:66, NIV).

Moment: Christian education begins when children learn who God is and what it means to have a personal relationship with Jesus (salvation).

Acquire: First Bible. (*Read with Me Bible* or *Beginner's Bible*)

Salvation: Introduce the need and lead the child to Christ as Savior (child asks to be part of His family, acknowledges sin and need for forgiveness)

Develop: A routine of Bible reading, prayer, and worship.

Attend: Regularly attend church and be enthusiastic about church life.

Promotion: Begin a new class at church.

Giving: Learn to give and serve (missions giving, too).

Friendships: Develop Christian relationships.

Evangelism: Develop non-Christian relationships in order to share Jesus.

Elementary (K–5th Grade)

Scripture: "The child grew and became strong in spirit, filled with wisdom; and the grace of God was upon Him" (Luke 2:40, NKJV).

Moment: Christian education continues: children learn more about who God is, grow deeper in their personal relationship with Jesus and how to follow Him, and are encouraged to start serving.

Promotion: Begin Kids Church and Wednesday evening—worship services at a child's level, experiencing God's presence.

Assurance of Salvation: **C**onfess Christ as Savior, re-commitment.

Acquire: *Adventure Bible* or *The Action Bible.*

Develop: **A** routine of prayer, worship, church attendance, giving

Attend: **C**amps and conferences.

Baptism: **A**ttend Baptism Class, get baptized in water.

Baptism: Get baptized in the Holy Spirit and receive a prayer language.

Serving: Volunteer in a ministry, serve at an event.

Friendships: Develop Christian relationships.

Evangelism: Invite others to church and/or lead a friend to Christ.

Faith-Building Between Church and Home

To help parents be more involved in the Christian education process of their children, we have designed our program to include both parents and guardians.

Worship

We invite parents to worship and pray with their child and encourage parents to plan a visit to their child's class at least two times a year or more. We also encourage parents to invite their kids to worship together with them whenever possible. Faith is caught, not always taught.

Grow

We encourage parents to join a small group with parents of kids in the same age or grade group. We ask parents to review their child's take-home papers with them weekly and to talk through the recommended discussion questions. Take-home papers let the parents know what Bible personalities and stories their children are studying at church. We encourage parents to ask about what their child has learned in a service or class, using open-ended questions.

Serve

We invite parents to serve once a month as Parent Partners in their child's class or another area within kids' ministries. We also encourage parents to volunteer and serve together as a family. Parent Partners do not replace teachers, but are an addition to the team. Parent Partners add strength and security, helping to provide an inviting atmosphere for new families. The parents' role is to help the teaching team to accomplish the goal of spiritual formation in the children.

Events

Children grow spiritually and develop Christian relationships that can strengthen their faith-journey at events. Events often act as a "spiritual greenhouse" for kids to grow deeper in their relationship with God. We encourage parents to invest in their child's spiritual growth by planning for these events by marking them on their calendars early and budgeting for them so their children can attend. This takes intentionality and communication on the part of the children's pastor or leader. In order to help parents plan, we share a full year's calendar at each of the Parent Previews, and we share the value we believe these events can add to their child's growth. Some of these events are: kids' conferences, kids' camp, outreach opportunities, and service projects that the whole family can engage in.

Church Traditions

Communion and Water Baptism

"Water Baptism and Communion embody the Christian faith. Water baptism is a one-time event in which the new believer announces publicly that he is now a child of God who has identified with Jesus Christ and His death and resurrection. Communion is a periodic reminder that the believer has received his free salvation through the suffering, death, and resurrection of Jesus Christ."[85]

I believe kids can understand and participate in both baptism and communion once they have invited Jesus to be their Lord and Savior. As a children's pastor I want nothing more than to see every child dedicated to the Lord, baptized in water, and understanding and participating in communion before they get promoted into youth ministries.

With that said, however, I recommend partnering with the parents to ensure these ceremonies are understood, meaningful,

---

[85] "What We Believe." Water of Life Assembly of God (http://www.wolag.net/what-we-believe.html).

and remembered by the child. I also recommend your church set some guidelines for children who are going to participate in either ordinance. Here are some practical tips to help you determine how to establish a few guidelines.

Baby-Child Dedication

Ted Weis, a pastor of the Congregational Church in Little River, Kansas beautifully outlines information about Baby-Child Dedication:[86]

> There's no greater moment [than] when parents sense that children are a gift from God. In these joyful moments, pastors have the privilege of sharing how parents can express their full appreciation to God and publicly acknowledge their desire to raise the child in the knowledge of the Lord than through baby dedication. . . .
>
> Dedicating a child acknowledges God's sovereignty not only over the child, but also Mom and Dad. Parents present their child before God and His people, asking for grace and wisdom in carrying out their responsibilities. Parents also come praying that their child might one day trust Jesus Christ as Savior for the forgiveness of sin.
>
> Before the actual ceremony, it is crucial that pastors counsel parents about the meaning of dedication. . . . This is a good time to query parents about their own personal relationship with Christ. . . .

Pastors should make clear that the duty of teaching children belongs to parents; church can provide weekly instruction, but parents must seize the teachable moments that arise throughout life.

---

[86] Ted Weis, "Baby Dedication." Bible.org. (https://bible.org/article/baby-dedication).

This is also the perfect time to invite them to the next Parent Orientation, to learn practical ideas they can incorporate into their daily family routines to provide spiritual formation for their child.

Each baby dedication is unique. Look for ways to customize each dedication according to the family. At the end of the ceremony we provide a certificate of dedication along with a parenting book, as a way to remember the spiritual milestone and encourage the parents to be the spiritual leaders in their home.

Water Baptism

At what age will a child understand water baptism? We know that every child develops at a different pace and, therefore, most children will be prepared for baptism at a different age. However, I also feel that it is important to establish a general baseline for the families of your church. I have personally set a baseline for water baptism at age seven; this is old enough for the child to mentally and spiritually comprehend what the Bible instructs about water baptism and to complete the water baptism application. This packet includes a teaching built around Scripture and includes worksheets to be completed by the child. It is important that children be old enough to answer these questions themselves; this provides a natural filter to determine those who are ready for water baptism. When you review the child's answers, with the parents present, it is always clear whether or not the child is ready for water baptism.

Second, we ask that parents or guardians attend the Kids Baptism Class with their child. We then ask questions and interact with each child, helping the parents to see firsthand whether or not their child is ready for this next step in obedience to Christ. If it is evident that a child is not ready, we communicate this to the parents and ask them to wait for a season and attend another class in six months or the following year. Ultimately, it is *not* solely the parents' decision, nor that of the children's pastor or leader. Rather, this partnering gauges each child individually to see if they are ready. We communicate that our desire is for their child to take this next step, but we want them to fully understand its meaning and remember the moment, so as not to have them come back as youth or adults and say, "I was too young to remember" or "I really didn't understand what I was doing." We want kids to experience a memorable God-moment, not just a ritual.

Lastly, after the child has taken the class and his or her application has been reviewed, the children's pastor or leader makes his or her recommendation to the pastoral team for final approval. Once that has happened, the parents are notified and the following week the child can be baptized!

Communion

When communion is offered at any service we coach the parents to instruct and lead their kids through this time. We ask parents to determine when their child is ready to receive communion and do not provide too many guidelines regarding age or level of maturity. We remind parents of this before the elements of communion are passed out, so that parents can decide beforehand if they will allow their child to partake of communion or not. We do teach about communion in our elementary kids' church setting, and if we are going to actually offer the communion elements to the kids there, we would first let the parents know beforehand through more than one way of written communication. This allows parents to guide their kids and help the parents to make the best decision for their children in advance.

SUMMARY

Partnering with parents in the spiritual growth of their children is both challenging and rewarding. Seeing parents encourage and lead their children to experience all God has for them and then celebrating those special milestones is fulfilling. We can see that each step of a child's faith-journey builds upon another and that our role as a children's pastor or leader is one of cheerleader, teacher, and resource-provider to parents. From seeing children read in their first Bible to being baptized in water, let's continue to do all that we can to partner with parents in the spiritual formation of their children and celebrate with them.

Reflection Questions

1. In what ways can I improve partnerships with parents in my church?
2. Has my church given frequent opportunities for kids to be dedicated to the Lord and baptized in water? Are guidelines in place? Is a class offered?
3. Have we been intentional in coaching parents to help lead their children to participate in communion?

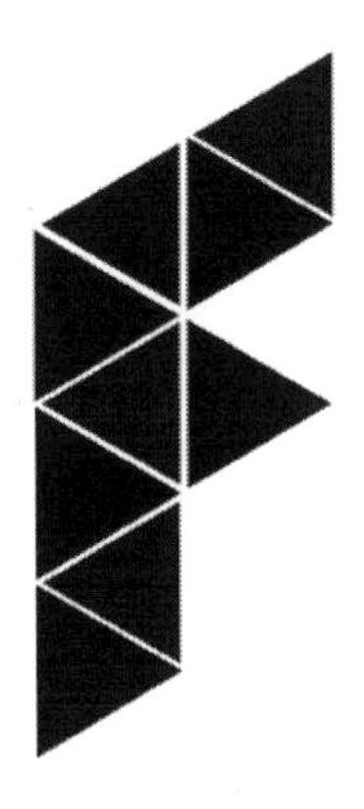

9.3 LEADING FROM THE MIDDLE

Jessica Downs

"Good leaders must first become good servants."
Robert K. Greenleaf

A true leader is not born overnight. Sure, a person might have God-given qualities that seem to put him or her naturally into a leadership role, but a *true* leader is developed over a long period of time. In all honesty, I'm not sure a leader is ever done growing. That's the thing about good leaders; even though they may manage a large group of people, they recognize that they still have a lot to learn from those around them. As humans, we learn best when we do, and we do best when we are willing to serve.

The servant-leader is not a new concept. In fact, we see a very real example of servant-leadership in Christ himself. He was fully God and fully man, yet he recognized his role was to serve the Father. He was pretty outspoken about it too, even as early as twelve years old.[87] In the same way, your position as a children's pastor is not one of first-chair leadership, but rather of support. You are, first and foremost, a follower. Of Christ, yes, but also of your senior pastor.

Submission is defined as accepting or yielding to the will of another person. You have to recognize that God placed your pastor in the position he is in and gave him a passion and vision for the people he leads.[88] Your pastor chose *you* to serve with him. Maybe he hired you or maybe he kept you on when he came; it doesn't really make a difference. He has entrusted his heart for the people to you. That is a huge level of responsibility he believes you can handle or else you wouldn't be there.

Now that we've covered the fact your pastor stands behind you, we need to talk about you standing behind him. I imagine we probably agree it is important, but what does true support look like? And how do you do it well? Supporting your pastor is a process of choosing contentment where you are, learning to speak his language, and then speaking it. Simply put, be present, be a student, and be an encourager.

Be Present

The first step of being a successful support to your pastor is to be where you are. Really be there. That sounds simple, but it's not. It is easy to allow your mind to wander, dwelling on the past or longing for the future. When that happens, though, we permit seeds of discontentment to take root. The search for contentment is

---

[87] Larry Spears, "The 10 Gifts of a Servant Leader." Daily Good: News That Inspires, June 4, 2013 (http://www.dailygood.org/story/447/the-10-gifts-of-a-servant-leader-larry-spears/).

[88] For simplicity's sake, I will refer to lead pastors as "he," though women make awesome lead pastors.

something that has plagued humans from the beginning of time. Go back to the Garden of Eden. Everything was perfect and yet Satan's ammunition against Adam and Eve was the desire for something more, something greater.[89]

We all know that the old adage "the grass is always greener on the other side of the fence" is farfetched, yet we tend to believe it when it comes to ministry. Whether it's the belief that getting volunteers is easier when you've got a bigger church or wishing your pastor would be more hands-off or hands-on, every church will have its challenges. That's because you aren't perfect and neither are the people you work with.

Contentment isn't just about where you are. True contentment stems from who you are. One of the most important things for us to grasp as believers is that we belong to the Lord. Our value has nothing to do with where we or what we do; it rests in whose we are. This doesn't give us a free pass on self-improvement, but it does give us a peace that goes beyond the here and now. As Theodore Roosevelt once said, "Comparison is the thief of joy." When we take our eyes off the One who has given us our purpose in order to focus the purpose of others, it won't take long to be stripped of our joy.

Commit yourself instead to becoming all God wants you to be where you are now. We learn in God's Word to not despise the day of small beginnings.[90] Receive this moment as a gift and seek to learn all you can where you are. God does not waste our time; He has a purpose in all of it. So choose to be faithful with what He has given you. Jesus said, "Whoever can be trusted with very little can also be trusted with much" (Luke 16:10, NIV).

---

[89] Zondervan, *NIV*, pt. Genesis 3.
[90] Ibid., pt. Zechariah 4:10.

You won't be able to fully support your pastor if you resent your position or constantly compare yourself with others. The enemy would love nothing more than to come in and knock you off course. Don't give him the opportunity. As they say, "Contentment is not the fulfillment of what you want, but the realization of how much you already have."

BE A STUDENT

The next step in becoming your pastor's biggest fan is to become a student. Learning to follow when you are a natural-born leader can be hard, especially when your leader has a different leadership style from yours. To truly support your pastor, you need to release him from your expectations. You can't assume he will do things the way you would; God has wired him differently. That's the beauty of the body of Christ—we all bring unique strengths to the table. Instead of seeing your differences as a nuisance, see them for what they are: an opportunity to learn from one another and be stronger together.

The best way to do that is to become a student of your pastor. Do you know your pastor's vision? Do you have a clear understanding of his expectations when it comes to your role in the church? And perhaps even more importantly, do you know his heart?

One of the things I appreciate most about my pastor is that he truly cares about people. He has built a culture of relationship; he calls it the "Ministry of Presence." When someone in our church is going through a difficult time, whether it be a sprained ankle or a cancer diagnosis, our pastors are there to provide encouragement and prayer. We have a pastor on call every day of the week and we rotate weekends. We also have a thriving care ministry to the people of the community, giving backpacks to students in August, turkeys to families in November, and presents to others in December, not to mention a foster care ministry that puts on camps throughout the summer.

It's not only important to know your pastor's heart; you need to learn to think the way your pastor thinks. What does he like and dislike? What does he value most in the workplace? Is it punctuality? Professionalism? The details aren't always spelled out in the new-hire packet and you might have to do some digging, but I can guarantee that it will only improve your relationship with your pastor. In fact, if you're still not sure, just ask!

One of the most valuable things my mentor, Jim Wideman, challenged me to do was to ask my pastor what a good children's pastor looks like. I took notes and came away with a very clear outline of his expectations. If I am ever unsure, I can refer back to it.

Ask yourself: What does being supported look like to your pastor? It might not match what you're doing and, to be frank, if he ain't feelin it, you ain't doin it right. I was introduced to a fantastic resource called the Path Elements Profile Test, or PEP.[91] It has dramatically changed how I work with and view those around me. It is similar to a DISC profile but it's easier to remember and understand, at least for me.

The test uses four elements of nature to explain how each of us is wired differently: water, earth, wind, and fire. A "Water" is someone who is very relationally driven and loyal. Someone who is an "Earth" is task driven and detail oriented. A "Wind" is outgoing and excited about what's next. A naturally wired "Fire" is someone who is a visionary and passionate. Each personality has strengths and weaknesses, and each one speaks a different language.

---

[91] Laurie Beth Jones, Jones, "The Path Elements Profile for Groups." (http://lauriebethjones.com/product/path-elements-profile-pep-for-groups).

I can tell you this - the sooner you learn to speak your pastor's language, the better. You'll avoid a lot of frustration on both sides if you show support the way he can receive it. You have to be willing to be a student of your pastor.

Be an Encourager

Once you know *how* to show support to your pastor, go and do it. Be a Barnabas. Barnabas is known as the "son of encouragement" in Acts. Everywhere he went he spoke life to those he served—both to those in authority over him and those he led. He served with Paul and believed in him, even when no one else did.[92] Barnabas went out of his way to bring Paul to Antioch to become the leader of the people.

Even more importantly, throughout Acts, we see Barnabas' willingness to step back so that Paul could step up into his God-given role. Barnabas doesn't seek the limelight but instead supports Paul in all he does.

Are you a Barnabas to your pastor? Or are you a thorn in his flesh? Ouch, right? Think about it for a moment. . . . If someone asked your pastor, would he say that you are an encouragement to him or that you stand in opposition to what he's trying to accomplish? I'm sure we'd all like to think that the answer would be the former, but you might want to take inventory. How do you speak about him in private? What does your non-verbal language say in public?

If you've been guilty of focusing on the negative rather than applauding the positive, ask God to help you learn how to speak your pastor's language of encouragement. Once you have the

---

[92] See Zondervan, *NIV*, pt. Acts 9:26-27.

information, act accordingly. And let your behavior be the same outside the office as it is on the inside.

That's not to say you won't have disagreements behind closed doors. In fact, healthy conflict is part of a working relationship. But choose which battles are worth fighting, because not all of them are. Unless it is a disagreement about foundational beliefs, there will be times when you have to come under the authority that he has been given and stand with him.

Even when you disagree on the "hows" of ministry, you should always speak well of your pastor. It may be human nature to want to complain to friends or your spouse about work because everyone else does, but you have to remember that your job is their church. Your boss is their pastor. There has to be a degree of separation; otherwise people will take up an offense that isn't theirs to bear. It can lead to disunity and even destruction.

Remember that you are a representative of your pastor and your church in all you do—when you visit people at the hospital, when you talk to people inside or outside your church, and every time you post on social media. Though your pastor is not responsible for your actions, your behavior is a reflection of him because he has *chosen you* to serve alongside him.

Go out of your way to encourage your pastor, in public and in private. Being a lead pastor is no walk in the park. My dad has been a senior pastor for twenty-five years, and though he's done a great job of guarding our hearts, I know the toll it can take on someone. Your pastor needs to hear your words of life. Write him a card, invite his family over for dinner, listen to his sermons and let him know what spoke to you. Pray God's blessing and protection over him. He is human and needs affirmation, just as you do.

CONCLUSION

In the end, supporting your pastor is more than showing up for work each day and sporting a coffee mug with your church logo; you have to believe in him. And in those moments when it's a little more difficult, ask the Lord for an extra measure of grace. You need to be able to love one another, even on your worst days.

I want you to know that I am writing this out of weakness. I'm not there yet. I make mistakes and I stick my foot in my mouth almost daily, but I also recognize the importance of this topic. A church cannot be healthy until the second tier of leadership is in support of the first.

In his book *Children's Ministry Leadership*, Jim Wideman reminds us, "Other than your mother, there's nobody in the world who wants to see you succeed in your ministry to kids more than your senior pastor."[93] You may have a pastor who seems over-critical, but when it comes down to it, know that he is trying to help. He is called by God to mentor and lead you. Receive his instruction with gratitude, not resentment, because he believes in you. If he didn't, you wouldn't still be where you are.

Most of all, don't allow the enemy to gain a foothold in your heart. Jesus said, "If a house is divided against itself, that house cannot stand."[94] We have to be in unity with our leadership or our ministry *will* fail; it's not a question of *if,* but *when*.

---

[93] Jim Wideman, *Children's Ministry Leadership*, 119.
[94] Mark 3:25, NIV

Reflection Questions

1. Without looking, write down the mission statement of your church. How did you do?
2. Write down twelve reasons why you are grateful to be at your church.
3. How can you determine which things are most important to your pastor? How well are you performing in those areas?
4. What are three things you can do in the next three weeks to show your support to your pastor?

ABOUT THE AUTHORS

Brent Colby

Brent Colby is really good at board games, reads lots of books, and drinks his espresso straight up. He has an incredible wife and four little kids that keep him busy when he is not serving as the Children's Ministry Director for the Northwest Ministry Network and Adjunct Professor of Children's Ministry at Northwest University. Until his rugby career takes off, Brent's primary goal is to develop leaders and make smart things.
brentcolby.com

Lauren Beach

Lauren Beach grew up in the great city of Everrett, Washington. She is an orange-loving, beach-going, coffee drinker who is passionate about seeing kids become more like Jesus. She graduated from Northwest University with a degree in Pastoral Ministries and an emphasis in Children's Ministry. She is an excellent leader in the local church and a key member of her church team.
facebook.com/laurenashleybeach

Nick Caalim

Nick and Stacy have been married since 2003 and have teamed up to raise five boys in Fircrest, WA. They have

served at Life Center in Pierce County since 2002. In their free time–let's be honest, they are raising five boys–there is no free time. But you can find them talking about Pixar movies or watching Mariners baseball.
twitter.com/NickACaalim

DAVE M. CAMERON

Dave M. Cameron serves as the Children's Pastor at Cedar Park Church in Bothell, Washington. Prior to serving as a children's pastor, he taught Secondary Bible classes at Cedar Park Christian School. Dave loves to teach and preach the word of God and help empower the next generation of believers to become men and women of God. Dave and his wife Johanna have three wonderful children ages seven, five and two.

JESSICA DOWNS

Jessica Downs is a Children's Pastor in the greater Seattle area with a passion to see kids God, not just know about Him. She graduated Northwest University in 2010 where she studied Kids Ministry and Missions. Jessica and her husband, Loren, have a heart for foster care and live to share Christ's love with kids.
twitter.com/MrsDowns11

DORENE HEETER

Dorene loves kids and their families. Her heart is to develop leaders and teams to serve the church, especially in the area

of children's ministries. She enjoys networking and has had many opportunities to inspire other children's ministries leaders around the world. Dorene's passion is to make the church a place where kids can have fun, but also experience the presence and transforming power of God. Dorene is an ordained minister and children's pastor that has served in the Pacific Northwest since 1989. She has 2 sons and a super-supportive husband, Bill.
twitter.com/dorenesmiles

Dan Metteer

Dan Metteer is a campus pastor who loves ultimate frisbee and disc golf. He serves as an Adjunct Professor of Children's Ministry at Northwest University and is devoted to the cause of children's ministry. Dan is driven by a passion to see the next generation of leaders respond to God's call on their lives. Dan married up and has three creative kids who do their best to keep up with dad.
twitter.com/danmetteer

Jace Murray

Jace Murray has a decade of experience in children's ministry and spent many years as a child when he was younger. He is personally invested into the development of crazy ideas to inspire an entire generation of kids. Jace likes to invest into passionate people, challenge traditional thinking, and write about himself in third person. Before working with kids, he served as a U.S. Marine which was surprisingly similar to working with kids. Through this experience and others, Jace has learned to take life seriously, but never himself. Also, let the Wookiee win. twitter.com/jacemurray

Bryan Reeder

Bryan Reeder has over 15 years of pastoral experience. He earned his B.A. in Church Ministries from Southwestern University and is an ordained minister with the Assemblies of God. Bryan and Jalita have been married since 1999, and they have three kids: Isaac, Austin, and Emma. twitter.com/bryankreeder

WORKS CITED

"A Brief History of Mpact Girls Clubs | Mpact Girls Clubs." *National Girls Ministry*. Accessed October 10, 2016. http://mgc.ag.org/about/history/.

A.B.C. News. "'Fight Church,' Christian Ministries Believe in Fight Clubs." *ABC News*, October 6, 2014. http://abcnews.go.com/US/jesus-throw-punches-fight-church-christian-ministries-fight/story?id=25953786.

Anthony, Michelle. *Spiritual Parenting: An Awakening for Today's Families*. New edition. Colorado Springs, CO: David C. Cook, 2010.

Atwood, Craig D., ed. *Handbook of Denominations in the United States*. 13 edition. Nashville: Abingdon Press, 2010.

Baird, Greg. *The Future of Children's Ministry*. Colorado Springs, CO: KidMin360. Accessed October 10, 2016. http://www.faithformationlearningexchange.net/uploads/5/2/4/6/5246709/the-future-of-childrens-ministry.pdf.

Botkin, Isaac, and Heidi Botkin. "The Spread of the Gospel Map." Accessed October 20, 2016. http://westernconservatory.com/products/the-spread-of-the-gospel-map.

Buckingham, Michael. "WTF Church." *Church Marketing Sucks*, September 6, 2010. http://www.churchmarketingsucks.com/2010/09/wtf-church/.

Carr, Nicholas. *The Shallows: What the Internet Is Doing to Our Brains*. W. W. Norton & Company, 2011.

Church, Methodist Episcopal. *The Catechism of the Methodist Episcopal Church: Numbers One, Two and Three*. Kessinger Publishing, LLC, 2010.

Ciment, James. *Social Issues in America: An Encyclopedia*. Vol. Volume 8. Routledge, 2015.

Eadicicco, Lisa. "Americans Check Their Phones 8 Billion Times a Day." *Time*, December 15, 2015. http://time.com/4147614/smartphone-usage-us-2015/.

Fenton Lee, Amy. "The Inclusive Church." *Leading a Special Needs Ministry Book to Be Available Again*. Accessed October 10, 2016. https://theinclusivechurch.wordpress.com/.

Gertz, Steven. "From Beer to Bibles to VBS." *ChristianityToday.com*. Accessed October 10, 2016. http://www.christianitytoday.com/ct/2003/juneweb-only/6-30-43.0.html.

Godin, Seth. *Free Prize Inside: How to Make a Purple Cow*. Reprint edition. New York: Portfolio, 2007.

House, GPH Gospel Publishing. *Royal Rangers Leader Manual: Inspire the Journey*. GPH, 2013.

Howe, Neil, and William Strauss. *Millennials Rising: The Next Great Generation*. 3rd Printing edition. New York: Vintage, 2000.

Jones, Dr Troy H. *Recalibrate Your Church: How Your Church Can Reach Its Full Kingdom Impact*. CreateSpace Independent Publishing Platform, 2016.

Jones, Laurie Beth. "The Path Elements Profile for Groups." *Laurie Beth Jones*. Accessed October 10, 2016. http://lauriebethjones.com/product/path-elements-profile-pep-for-groups.

Keller, Timothy. *Center Church: Doing Balanced, Gospel-Centered Ministry in Your City*. 8.9.2012 edition. Grand Rapids, MI: Zondervan, 2012.

"Kentucky Baptist Church Gun Giveaway Draws People To 'Second Amendment Celebrations.'" *The Huffington Post*. Accessed August 26, 2016. http://www.huffingtonpost.com/2014/03/03/kentucky-baptist-church-gun-giveaway_n_4890017.html.

Lyons, Gabe. *The Next Christians: The Good News About the End of Christian America*. New York: Doubleday Religion, 2010.

Martin, David. *Pentecostalism: The World Their Parish*. 1 edition. Oxford ; Malden, Mass: Wiley-Blackwell, 2001.

McGee, Gary B., Charles M. Self, and George O. Wood. *People of the Spirit*. Revised edition. Gospel Publishing House, 2014.

Nale, Billy. *The Sunday School as a Viable Tool for Church Growth in the 21st Century*. ProQuest, 2007. http://books.google.com/books?hl=en&lr=&id=G4UAcnmSXPgC&oi=fnd&pg=PA1&dq=%22the+Organization%22+%22School+Needs+to+be+Flexible%22+%22Class+Organization%22+%22School+Organization%22+%22School+Workers+Meetings%22+%22and+Enrolling+Prospects%22+%225+-+First+Baptist+Church,+Gulf+Shores,+Alabama%22+&ots=0jgZwuQQl7&sig=0LVSPdjA83-MtagUG6XnpZDklp8.

Peters, Edward. *A Modern Guide to Indulgences: Rediscovering This Often Misinterpreted Teaching*. LiturgyTrainingPublications, 2008.

Powell, Kara E., Chap Clark, and John Ortberg and Jim Candy. *Sticky Faith: Everyday Ideas to Build Lasting Faith in Your Kids*. Grand Rapids, Mich: Zondervan, 2011.

Rainer, Thom S. *Effective Evangelistic Churches*. B&H Academic, 1996.

Rosenberg, Hugh. "Lead Your Children." *Pentecostal Evangel*, June 17, 2012. http://www.pe.ag.org/articles/index_2012.cfm?targetBay=f5f8225a-e34d-4383-8e42-e3b9d80d8a4d&ModID=2&Process=DisplayArticle&RSS_RSSContentID=22988&RSS_OriginatingChannelID=1321&RSS_OriginatingRSSFeedID=4907&RSS_Source.

Rosenberg, Hugh, and Brad Rosenberg. "Father Print." *Father Print*. Accessed October 10, 2016. http://fatherprint.com/.

Spears, Larry. "The 10 Gifts of a Servant Leader." *Daily Good: News That Inspires*, June 4, 2013. http://www.dailygood.org/story/447/the-10-gifts-of-a-servant-leader-larry-spears/.

Stephany, Marie. "Mother Peace." *Assemblies of God Heritage* 17, no. 4 (1997): 36.

Tanner, Jeri. "A Brief History of Sunday School." *Ministry to Children*, October 12, 2009. http://ministry-to-children.com/history-of-sunday-school/.

"The History of BGMC." *Boys and Girl's Missionary Challenge*. Accessed October 10, 2016. http://bgmc.ag.org/about/history/.

"The State of Vacation Bible School." *Barna Group*. Accessed October 10, 2016. https://www.barna.com/research/the-state-of-vacation-bible-school/.

Thomas, Darren W. "The Role, History, and Decline of Sunday School," 2005. http://eridan.websrvcs.com/clientimages/36689/historyofthesundayschool.pdf.

Tyndale. *Holy Bible : New Living Translation*. 0002–edition ed. Wheaton, Ill.: Tyndale House Publishers, Inc., 2004.

Weddle, Linda. "Trends in Children's Ministry." *Kidzmatter.com*, December 27, 2013. http://kidzmatter.com/trends-in-childrens-ministry/.

Weis, Ted. "Baby Dedication." *Bible.org*. Accessed October 10, 2016. https://bible.org/article/baby-dedication.

Wesley, John. *Wesley's Revision Of The Shorter Catechism - Primary Source Edition*. Nabu Press, 2014.

"What We Believe." *Water Of Life Assembly of God*. Accessed October 10, 2016. http://www.wolag.net/what-we-believe.html.

Wideman, Jim. *Children's Ministry Leadership: The You-Can-Do-It Guide*. Loveland, CO: Group Publishing, 2003.

Wightman, William May. *Life of William Capers*. Publishing House of the ME Church, South, 1902.

Winter, Ralph, and Steven Hawthorne. *Perspectives on the World Christian Movement: Reader and Study Guide - eBook*. 4 edition. William Carey Library, 2014.

Young, Ed, and Lisa Young. "7 Days to Lasting Intimacy." Accessed August 26, 2016. http://thesexperiment.com/about.

Zemeckis, Robert. *Back to the Future*. Adventure, Comedy, Sci-Fi, 1985.

Zimbalist, Andrew, Howard J. Sherman, and Stuart Brown. *Comparing Economic Systems: A Political Economic Approach*. 2 edition. San Diego: Harcourt College Pub, 1988.